2019
Bhajan Supplement

Mata Amritanandamayi Center, San Ramon
California, United States

2019 Bhajan Supplement

Published By:
Mata Amritanandamayi Center
P.O. Box 613
San Ramon, CA 94583-0613, USA

In India:
www.amritapuri.org
inform@amritapuri.org

In Europe:
www.amma-europe.org

In US:
www.amma.org

About Pronunciation

The following key is for the guidance of those who are unfamiliar with the transliteration codes used in this book:

A	-as	a	in America
AI	-as	ai	in aisle
AU	-as	ow	in how
E	-as	e	in they
I	-as	ea	in heat
O	-as	o	in or
U	-as	u	in suit
KH	-as	kh	in Eckhart
G	-as	g	in give
GH	-as	gh	in loghouse
PH	-as	ph	in shepherd
BH	-as	bh	in clubhouse
TH	-as	th	in lighthouse
DH	-as	dh	in redhead
CH	-as	ch-h	in staunch-heart
JH	-as	dge	in hedgehog
Ñ	-as	ny	in canyon
Ṣ	-as	sh	in shine
Ś	-as	c	in efficient
Ṅ	-as	ng	in sing, (nasal sound)
V	-as	v	in valley
ZH	-as	rh	in rhythm
R	-as	r	in ride

Vowels with a line on top are pronounced like the vowels listed above but held twice as long.
The letters with dots under them (ṭ, ṭh, ḍ, ḍh, ṇ) are palatal sounds. They are pronounced with the tip of the tongue against the hard palate.

Table of Contents

abhīṣṭavaradāyikē (Kannada version) 7
agragaṇya agrapūjya (Telugu) 7
ammā nī baruvēyā (Kannada) 8
ammā nī (Tamil) 9
amme kaṇṇu turakūle (Kannada version) 10
ammē manassiloru (Malayalam) 11
ānandam paramānandam (Telugu) 12
annay maḍiyil (Tamil) 13
anupamā nina (Kannada) 14
apārakṛpāḷō (Kannada) 15
apāra kṛpālō (Telugu) 16
ārati ambaku (Telugu) 17
aruṇaiyil (Tamil) 18
ayntu karattanai (Tamil) 19
brahmam okkaṭēyani (Telugu) 20
candraśēkharā (Telugu) 21
cintana ēla manasā (Telugu) 23
dāsōham (Telugu) 24
dayāvanta dṛṣṭi (Marathi) 25
ettanai murai (Tamil) 26
gaṇanāyakā devā (Marathi) 27
gaṇapati bāppā morayā (Marathi) 28
gōvinda gōpāla ani (Telugu) 30
govinda govinda (Tamil) 30
gōvinda jaya jaya jaya (namavali) 32
hṛdayātīl amūlya (Marathi) 32

oru nimisham (Tamil) 67
pañcēndriya (Kannada) 67
paripāvana (Marathi) 68
premasandāyini (Marathi) 69
prēmasūrya (Kannada) 70
puṇḍalika varadā (Marathi) 71
rāga vairikaḷ (Telugu translation) 73
rāmā jaya jaya rāmā (namavali) 74
sādi tōjāle (Tulu) 75
śēṣaśayana (Kannada) 76
sirikka connāḷ (Marathi version) 79
sirikka connāḷ (Tamil) 77
śivanenīnu (Kannada) 81
śiva śiva rudra śivā (Telugu) 82
Some say love (English) 83
śrī rāma rāma rāmetī (Marathi) 84
śrīvāri pādālu (Telugu) 85
tāḷ paṇintōm (Tamil) 87
tāyillā piḷḷayō (Tamil) 88
tiruvaḍi pukazhppāḍa (Tamil) 88
vāzhkaiyoru (Tamil) 89
vinavite (Marathi) 91
yellā daiva ondē (Kannada) 92
yēnu mahimē (Kannada) 93

iruvudu eraḍē (Kannada) 34
jagamantalō (Telugu) 35
janani sakal (Hindi) 36
jaya jagadīśvarī (Marathi) 38
jaya janani caitanya (Telugu) 39
jhevhā vāṭṭ (Marathi) 40
kāḷi karuṇākarī (Tamil) 41
kaṇṇanu naivēdyam (Malayalam) 43
kēśava bēgane (Kannada) 44
mahāmāyi mahākāḷi (Telugu) 45
manadinuḷḷil (Tamil) 46
mandahāsavadane (namavali) 47
mantirattirkkilla (Tamil) 48
manuṣyan-iviḍe (Malayalam) 49
māyē embāḷatā (Kannada) 50
mōḍa musukide (Kannada) 51
muttamizh-nāyakī (Tamil) 51
muttu muttu vēlavanē (Tamil) 53
nāce tū (Hindi) 54
nā eda kōvelalō (Telugu) 56
nallanivāḍu (Telugu) 57
nām ek rūp (Hindi) 58
nanda nandanā (Tamil) 59
nānu nānallavembante (Kannada) 62
nijavan ariyadē (Kannada) 63
nijava nariyadē (Telugu version) 64
nīlavaṇṇā (Tamil) 65
oru nalil nyan (Tamil) 66

abhīṣṭavaradāyikē (Kannada version)

abhīṣṭavaradāyikē jñānasukhadāyikē
janmaphaladāyikē bandū
hṛdayadi nelesammā kamalāmbikē

nenappugaḷ udayisida dinadindanā ninna
ārādhanāpuṣpa vā gihēnu
sāvirārubhā va gītegaḷinda ninna
nannanta rangadalli huḍukkuttidde – mana
ārdravāgī pari tapissuttiddu

hṛdayava hiṇḍuva bhaktibhā vēśa
pathadalli ēkānta pathikkeyāgi nā
ondondu hūvinallū ondondu meghadallū
araḷuva ninmukha nōḍinintē – ammā
nannanē marēttunā nōḍi nintē

agragaṇya agrapūjya (Telugu)

agragaṇya agrapūjya ēkadantasvāmī
vakratuṇḍa mahākāya gaṇapati śubhanāma

O foremost One, who is always worshipped first; You have a single-tusk and an elephant head with a curved-trunk. Your body is great, O Ganapati, and Your name is auspicious.

śaraṇam gaṇēśā śaraṇam gaṇēśā
śaraṇam gaṇēśā śaraṇam śaraṇam

O Ganesha, we take refuge in You!

modaṭipūja nī mūrttikē cēsēmu nāthā
ābālagōpālam cētturu nī gānam
karivadanā kamalanētrā karuṇasvarūpā

We offer our first prayers to You. Everyone, from young to old, poor to rich, sings Your song. You have the face of an elephant and Your eyes are like that of a lotus; You are the embodiment of compassion.

mōdamutō mōdakālu arppintumu svāmi
lambōdara nīnāmam nityam namāmi
karivadanā kamalanētrā karuṇasvarūpā

O Lord, we joyfully offer You modaka (a sweet dish). Big-bellied One, we always chant Your name. You have the face of an elephant and Your eyes are like that of a lotus; You are the embodiment of compassion.

ammā nī baruvēyā (Kannada)

ammā nī baruvēyā
karuṇāmṛta harisuvēyā
mana tumbi nā karēdaru
taḍa vēkē nī baralu

O Mother, will you come and shower the nectar of your compassion on me? I have been fervently calling out to you, why do you delay in coming?

jñānada dīpava beḷagisalu
nānemba bhāvava hōgisalu
ninnapāda padmagaḷē ēkāśraya
ninna maḍilallē kāṇuvē abhaya

Your lotus feet are my only hope to light the lamp of knowledge and remove the sense of 'I'; I seek refuge in your lap.

ninna divyanāma smaraṇayalli
mañjinantē enmana karagali
śaraṇu bandihēnu ninna pādakkē
appi koḷḷalu taḍa ētakē

Let my heart melt like a snowflake in the remembrance of your divine name. Your feet are my sanctuary, why do you not embrace me in your arms?

sṛṣṭiyum nīnē sṛṣṭāvum nīnē
śivanu nīnē śaktiyum nīnē
ādiyum nīnē antyavu nīnē
kaṇakaṇadallu nīnē nīnē

You are Shiva. You are Shakti. You are the creation and the creator. You are the beginning and the end. You are present in each and every atom.

ammā nī (Tamil)

ammā nī ennai marantatēnō?
marantu viṭṭāl enna seyivēnō?

Mother, did you forget me? If You were to forget me, what would I do?

un vazhi pātaiyil kāttiruntēnē,
en vizhi mūṭāmal pārttiruntēnē
kaṇṇai maraittatu kaṇṇīr tirai
kaṇṇīr tuṭaikkum un karankaḷenkē?

Mother, I was waiting on your pathway. I was eagerly looking for you without even blinking my eyes. Tears welled up and filled my eyes. Mother, where are your hands to wipe away my tears?

ammā ammā ammā

O Mother

uḷḷattil vēdanai sērttu vaittēnē
unniṭam solla nān kāttiruntēnē
unnai kaṇḍatum pēccizhantēnē
ūmayin uḷḷattai arivāyō?

Mother, I have accumulated sorrows in my heart. I was waiting to share them with you, but when I saw you, I became speechless. Mother, don't you know my heart even as I remain silent?

amme kaṇṇu turakūle (Kannada version)

ammā kaṇṇuteraye amma
andhatē nīgisē bārammā
ādaradinda akhaṇḍanāmava
āpādadī nā arppisuvē

ajñānigaḷā lōkavidammā
ajñatē nīgalu yāriharu
vijñānada mahā mukuṭamaṇi nī
viśvamahāmayi dayamāḍu

bhaktapriyē nī bhuvanēśvari nī
bhaktaramēle dayētōru
karajōḍisuta namisuva makkaḷa
kaṭākṣa bīri kāppāḍu

saptarṣigaḷu ninnanu stutiparu
sūktava hāḍi naliyuvaru

taptamanassina manujaru nāvu
śaktimahāmayi kāppāḍu

ammē manassiloru (Malayalam)

ammē manassiloru pūkkaḷam tīrkkunnu
nī vannirikkumō ennumennum
ammē vāḍāmalar māla korukkunnu
nīyaṇaññīṭumō ennumennum

Mother, will you come and be enshrined forever and ever in the pukkalam (beautiful intricate pattern of flowers) that you have etched in my heart? Mother, I weave a garland for you with fresh flowers. Will you adorn yourself with it forever and ever?

ennumī kaṇṇīru vattātozhukunnu
nin pāda padmatteyācamikkān
ennum śirassu kuniññukoṇḍē nilpu
nin pādarēṇuveḍuttu tūvān

My tears flow incessantly to wash your lotus feet. I forever bow down before you, that I may be blessed by the dust of your feet.

sarva duḥkhaṅgaḷum sarva mōhaṅgaḷum
sarva sambattum ñān naivēdyamākkiyō
nityavum nēdippū, nī vanneṭukkilō
jīvannuruḷitan klāvum tiḷaṅgiṭum

I offer you all my sorrows, all my desires, all my wealth. I have been doing this forever- won't you come and accept my offerings, thus making my sorrows vanish and my life shine?

ennile vākkum satkarmavum cintayum
ennumē ninnekkuriccuḷḷatākaṇē
sarvavum vismariccuṇmaye tēṭuvān
nī kaniññēkumō nin stanyamādhuryam

May my words, deeds and thoughts forever be yours. Renouncing everything, I have come in search of you, Mother. Will you grant me the sweetness of mother's milk?

ānandam paramānandam (Telugu)

ānandam paramānandam
saccidānandam niratiśayānandam

Bliss, supreme bliss, pure consciousness bliss, incomparable bliss.

rāmarasamidi migula tīyani
pānamu sēyaga ānandam
rāmamayamī jagamani teliyaga
bhaktajanulaku ānandam
rāmanāmamidi tārakamantramu
japamu sēya nityānandam

This is 'ramaras', sweetest of the sweetest, the drinking of which brings bliss. Devotees feel blissful, knowing that this world is full of Rama alone. The name of Rama will make you cross the ocean of samsara, chanting it brings bliss.

navarasabharitamu rāmacaritamu
ālakiñcaga ānandam
rāgarañjita punitagānamu
ālapiñcaga ānandam

rāmarūpamu antarangamuna
niṇḍukonaga ātmānandam

The story of Rama contains the nine rasas, listening to it brings bliss. The melodious singing of the holy narrative brings bliss. Filling your heart with Rama's form will make you feel blissful.

śrī rām jaya jaya rām
śrī rām rām rām rām
rām jay jay rām

Victory to Lord Rama!

annay maḍiyil (Tamil)

annay maḍiyil ōr kuzhandaiyāgalām
tāy maḍiyil sella piḷḷaiyāgalām
kuzhandai pōlavē uḷḷam punidamāgavē
manidan enbavan uyarndu daivamāgalām

Let us become a babe in Mother's lap. When the heart becomes as pure and pristine as an infant's, a human being can become divine.

annai nīṭṭum kaippiḍittu kūḍappōgalām
annay kāṭṭum pādai pintuḍarndu sellalām
piravu iravu taḍai kaḍandu uṇmai aḍayalām

Holding Mother's hand, let us walk with her. Let us follow the path she shows us. We can then transcend life and death, and attain the Truth.

uṇmai ariyavē inda manida janmamē
daivam tanda parisu tān embaduṇmayē
vēdamunivar yōginarum sonnadum iduvē

When we attain the Truth, we will realize that the human birth is a gift from God. So declared the rishis (seers) and yōgis (Self-realized souls).

bandhu enḍru solla ingu yārumillaiyē
sondam enḍru solli namba evarum illayē
sondam enḍrumē namakku annai oruvaḷē

There is no one here to call our own. There is no one we can trust enough to call our own. Only Mother is ever our own.

anupamā nina (Kannada)

anupamā nina bālalīle
gaṇapa ninage kai mugive
dēvagaṇa-gaḷa adhipane nīnu
bālagaṇapa kai mugive

Dear Lord Ganesha, the feats of your childhood are unparalleled. I bow down to You. I bow down to little Ganesha who is the leader of the devas (demi-gods).

śaktiputrane yuktipūrṇṇane
jāṇa gaṇapa kai mugive
śivana dvāradi śivana taḍeda
dhīra gaṇapa kai mugive

I bow down to the clever Ganesha, son of Goddess Parvati, who is very skillfull. I bow down to the brave Ganesha who was fearless enough to stop Shiva from entering his own home.

jagada mātā pitara sutti
jagava suttida phalava paḍēde
jagada mātā pitara nīnu

jagaku migilu entu karede
dhīra gaṇapa kai mugive

Circumambulating the Mother and Father of the Universe, You achieved the merit of circumambulating the entire Universe. You are the Mother and Father of all. I bow down to Ganesha who is greater than the Universe.

āne mukhada doḍḍa gaṇapa
puṭṭa iliya mēle kuḷittu
aṇuvu dēvane mahattu dēvane
brahmatattvava sārutiruve
dhīra gaṇapa kai mugive

O Ganesha, You are elephant-faced and have a large body (symbolizing strength, intelligence and ever listening to our calls). You are seated on a little mouse (keeping wandering senses under control). The smallest atom is You; the largest and greatest is also You. I bow down to the valiant Ganesha who is ever demonstrating to us the absolute Truth.

apārakṛpāḷō (Kannada)

apārakṛpāḷō baḷigenna bārō
avanīśvarā kṛṣṇā varavondu tāro
arivina hūnage araḷali manadali
anutāpa vagali ennātmakinde
kṛṣṇā

karuṇāpūrita sundara nayanadā
kāntiyu hṛnmana beḷagali bā
dahisuva hṛdayāntarāḷadi ondīsu
karuṇe maḷe hanise bēgane bā kṛṣṇā

maṇimuraḷikeyā nūduta bā
manamandiradi nī nalidāḍu bā
śrutilaya sangīta rasadhāre yondigē
matilaya sukhalābha gati nīḍu bā
kṛṣṇā

apāra kṛpālō (Telugu)

apāra kṛpālō nā darikki rāvā
avanīśvarā kṛṣṇā varamulu osagavā
virajāji navvunā śōka tapta madilōna
cirujallu kuripiñci vikasimpavā
kṛṣṇā

karuṇanu kuripiñcu nayanāla kāntitō
nā antarangamunu sparśiñcavā
tapiyiñcu hṛdayāntarāḷalō – svalpam
prēmarasāmṛtam varṣimpavā
kṛṣṇā

mṛdumuraḷī gāna paravaśamaina nā
manamandiramulō nāṭyamāḍa rā
śrutilaya sangīta rasa dhāratō nā
manassunu nīlō layam cēyyavā
kṛṣṇā

ārati ambaku (Telugu)

ārati ambaku hārati
ātma samarppaṇa hārati

O Goddess, through the auspicious arati, we surrender everything to you.

ahamu karpūramai karigē hārati
jñānamu jyōtigā veligē hārati
ammanu cūpē erukē hārati
jagamu ammagā kāñcē hārati

When the camphor of our ego burns during arati, it leaves behind no residue. The light of wisdom shines brightly. That light reveals the divine Mother and gives us the awareness that the whole universe is a manifestation of the divine Mother.

manalō nityamu veligē hārati
vāsanakṣayamu onarccē hārati
cittaśuddhiniccē prajñayē hārati
muktipathamuna diviṭi hārati

The arati glimmers eternally within as the inner spiritual light, which dispels the darkness of our latent tendencies. That light manifests as our highest awareness, which purifies the mind and illumines our way to spiritual liberation.

mangaḷam bhuvanēśvarī
mangaḷam jagadīśvarī
mangaḷam hṛdayēśvarī
mangaḷam sarvēśvarī

I offer the auspicious arati to the Goddess of the Earth, the Goddess of the Universe, the Goddess of my heart, and the Goddess of all (Goddess of Immortality).

aruṇaiyil (Tamil)

aruṇaiyil uraiyum karuṇai kaḍalē
taruṇam idu tān dayai purivāyē
umaiyoru bhāgam koṇḍa en śivanē
emaiyum tānkudal undan kaḍanē

O Shiva, self-effulgent One, ocean of compassion, please show mercy on me. Half of Your body is Goddess Uma- isn't it Your responsibility to hold on to us also?

namaḥ śivāya namaḥ śivāya
namaḥ śivāya om namaḥ śivāya

anal vaḍivāgiya ādiyām iraivā
punalai talayil cūḍiḍum talaivā
māl ayan kāṇā pēroḷi vaḍivē
mān uruvinaiyum karattinil koṇḍāy

O primordial Lord, who is in the form of fire, You adorn your head with the river Ganga. Even Brahma and Vishnu could not see You, You assumed the form of supreme light. You hold the deer in your hand (indicating that You are the controller of our mind, which jumps everywhere like the deer).

alaiyum manamum aḍankiḍa vēṇḍum
nilaiyām unpadam sērndiḍa vēṇḍum
vēdankaḷ pōttriḍum un uruvadanai
gītankaḷ pāḍi nān tudittiḍa vēṇḍum

Let my wavering mind become steady and calm. Let me reach Your feet which are the only unchanging haven. O Lord, Your form is praised by the vedas (scriptures), let me sing Your praises and worship You.

ayntu karattanai (Tamil)

ayntu karattanai pōṭriḍuvōm
yānai mukhattanai pōṭriḍuvōm
jñāla mutalvanai pōṭriḍuvōm
jñāna kozhuntinai pōṭriḍuvōm

Let us praise the one with five hands, let us sing the glories of the elephant-headed one! Let us glorify the Lord of the Universe! Let us praise the effulgent light of spiritual wisdom!

aravamaṇinta perumānai
makizhvuḍan pōṭrum malaimakaḷin
manamkavar maintan vēzhavanai
vaṇankiṭuvōmē ennāḷum

Pārvati—consort of Lord Shiva, adorned with a serpent around His neck—is ever engaged in glorifying Her Lord. We adore eternally the elephant-headed Lord who captivated Pārvati's heart.

paḍaippinirkkellam ādhāram
piḷḷaiyaipōlē ezhiyavanām
maṇṇil piḍittālum mañcaḷil piḍittālum
manamirankum ezhil vaḍivamavan

You are the substratum of the universe and yet as innocent as a child. Whether fashioned from clay or turmeric, You are still merciful, O Lord of enchanting form.

nallavarkkeṭṭum nallavanē
nambiyavarkku nattruṇayē
aḍankiya manatil aruḷ naḍamāḍum
adhipatiyē aḍiyār nidhiyē

O embodiment of goodness, You are easily attained by the virtuous. You are a refuge to those who have faith in You. The very embodiment of grace, You dance gracefully in tranquil minds.

brahmam okkaṭēyani (Telugu)

brahmam okkaṭē yani telisi-nantanē
brahma jñānivi kāvu kadā!
brahmānubhūti ponda kunḍanē
brahma jñānivi kāvu kadā!

Can one become a jñani (self-realized being), by the mere knowledge that Brahman alone exists? Can one become a Jñani without the experience of Self-Realization ?

pālu tellanani telisi-nantanē
pāluruci teliya rādu kadā!
āvu bōmmalu gīci nantanē
bōmmalu pālu ivvavu kadā!

Is it possible to know the taste of milk by knowing that it is white? Is it possible to get milk by simply drawing a picture of a cow?

vittu mokka ai vṛddhi kānidē
mahāvṛkṣamu kādu kadā!
cittamu śuddhi kalaga kunḍanē
brahma jñānamu rādu kadā!

Is it possible for a huge tree to emerge, without the seed first becoming a plant and growing? Is it possible to obtain supreme knowledge without first purifying the mind?

prēma bhaktini ponda kunḍanē
jñānamu nilaci pōdu kadā
amma kaṭākṣamu ponda lēnidē
amṛtānandamē lēdu kadā!

Is it possible to hold on to supreme knowledge when devoid of love and devotion? Is it possible to reach the state of eternal bliss without the grace of the divine Mother ?

jaya gōvindā jaya gōvindā
gōvindā jaya gōvindā
jaya jagadambā jaya jagadambā
jagadambā jaya jagadambā

So let us revel in the names of the divine: victory to Govinda, victory to the Mother of the Universe!

candraśēkharā (Telugu)

candraśēkharā nīlakandharā
phālolōcana pālayamām
pannagābharaṇa jaṭaladhāraṇā
bhasmabhūṣaṇa pālayamām

We take refuge in Lord Shiva, who wears the crescent moon on his head, has a blue-hued throat, and an eye on his forehead. We take refuge in him, who is adorned with a snake, wears matted locks, is smeared with ash.

kuriyajēyumā kṛpārasamunu
ninnēkoliceda nirantaramu
madini nimpavā bhaktibhāvamu
pāpanāśana santatamu

We constantly pray to you that you may shower your grace on us. O remover of sins, please fill our hearts with devotion.

dōṣahāraka duḥkhaduritamu
dariki rānē rānīyaku
trilōkapālaka ninne nammiti
mahāmāyalō muñcēyaku

Please mitigate the consequences of our wrong deeds. Do not let sorrow or suffering visit us. O ruler of the three worlds, I have taken refuge in you. Please do not let me drown in the sea of delusion.

naṭana manōhara naṭarājā
munivara sannuta mahādēvā
suravara vandita śubhakara śankara
purahara bhavahara parātparā
purahara bhavahara parātparā

O King of Dance, your dance is captivating. O Supreme Lord, you are glorified by the saints. O Auspicious One who bestows bliss, the gods pay obeisance to you. O greatest of the greats, you destroyed the three cities, and you help your devotees overcome the cycle of birth and death.

cintana ēla manasā (Telugu)

cintana ēla manasā centana
amma undigā marēmi

Why worry O mind, when Mother is near you?

karuṇatō niṇḍina ā kamala nētramulu
mikkili melakuvatō nī vennu kāyagā
cintanu vīḍi śāntini pondu
o manasā ammanu maruvaku

Those compassion-filled eyes are always vigilantly following you. Leave all worries and be at peace. O mind, don't forget Mother.

ēcōṭanunnanu ā kamala hastamulu
pottililō biḍḍagā lālistu uṇḍagā
cintanu vīḍi śāntini pondu
o manasā ammanu maruvaku

Wherever you are, those lotus hands will always be protecting you like a new born baby. Leave all worries and be at peace. O mind, dont forget Mother.

ellaraku abhayamu ā pādapadmamulu
śaraṇanna vāriki cērunu sadgatulu
cintanu vīḍi śāntini pondu
o manasā ammanu maruvaku

Those lotus feet offer refuge to everyone, and those who seek refuge will obtain salvation. Leave all worries and be at peace. O mind, dont forget Mother.

dāsōham (Telugu)

dāsōham amba dāsōham
dāsōham kāḷi dāsōham

O Divine Mother I am your servant! I am your servant O Kali!

baṇṭurīti koluvu iccina kāni
aham ēla cāvadē kāḷī
prati kāryamu nīvu cēsina kāni
kartta nēne anubhāvamu tolaga dēla kāḷi

O Kali, although I am blessed with the opportunity to serve you, why am I still not rid of my ego? Though You are the one doing all the work, why am I not rid of the feeling of doership, O Kali?

ambā nī dāsanu kāḷī nī dāsanu

O Divine Mother I am your servant! I am your servant O Kali!

nīdu sannidhi pondina kāni
māyā nannu vīḍadēla kāḷi
ambā dāsuḍani palikē nāku
śaraṇāgati ēla rādē kāḷi

Though I am blessed to be in your presence, why am I not rid of maya (the Illusory world) O Kali? Though I proclaim myself as your servant, why am I not able to fully surrender to you, O Kali?

kalmaṣa vāsanalu niṇḍina manasuku
śuddhata eppuḍu vaccune kāḷi
śraddhā bhakti viśvāsamulicci
nī caraṇa dāsuni rakṣiñcu janani

My mind is full of polluted tendencies and negativities. When will it become pure, O Kali? Bestowing awareness, devotion and faith please protect this servant of your lotus feet, O Mother!

dayāvanta dṛṣṭi (Marathi)

dayāvanta dṛṣṭī karī kṛpāvṛṣṭī
sāmāvalī tyāt samasta sṛṣṭī
nit vāhatī kāruṇyācyā laharī
vidhātrī tava nētrī jagadīśvarī

Your gaze, full of compassion, showers grace. Your eyes, full of affection, are like an ocean of love sporting the waves of mercy. Those eyes contain the whole universe.

samatva bhāv tuzā asē mahān
mamatva dēsī tū sarvāsī samān
tyā divya lōcanī athāng asē śāntī
pāhatā tayāsī lābhē santuṣṭī

People understand you according to their mental attitude. For you, though, all are equal. In your eyes, there is love for all. On seeing your gaze, the heart is content.

bhaktānvar phirē āī tuzhī nazar
uzaḷē antaḥ-ranga saratē timir
ānandācē hē kṣaṇ kartā jatan
miḷē bhaktī bhāv an prēm puṣṭī

When You gaze at devotees, the darkness of their inner self is dispelled. When those moments of happiness are preserved, the love and the devotion they feel for you are enhanced.

ānandaḍōhī tyā ākaṇṭha buḍāvē
sukha duḥkha sārē visarūnī zāvē
tujhē prēm karma ācaraṇī bhināvē
ambē nitya rāhō tava kṛpā dṛṣṭī

When one is completely immersed in those deep waters of bliss, one forgets all the sorrows and sufferings of worldly life. May Mother's love be reflected in our thoughts and actions. O Mother, may your compassionate gaze be ever on us.

ettanai murai (Tamil)

ettanai murai azhaittālum ennammā
ennarugē varādadum ēnammā
azhaippadu keṭkalayō tayirkkaḍaiyum pōdilē
azhugai varum munnē arukil varuvāyē
tāyē yaśōdammā

O Mother, why don't you come to me even though I've called you so many times? (Lord Krishna sings this song to his mother Yashōda.) Didn't you hear me call to you as you were churning the butter? Please come to me before I start crying. O Mother Yashoda!

maṇvīḍu muḍiyavillai kaṭṭa kaṭṭa uḍaigiradu
manidakula sinna sinna āsai pōlavē
kayyiraṇḍum kuzhaindu pasiyum vāṭṭudammā
kai niraya veṇṇaiyē aḷḷi aḷḷi taruvāyē
tāyē yaśōdammā

Like our petty desires, the mud house starts to crumble even before we can finish building it, leaving us disappointed. My hands are exhausted, and I am racked by hunger. Please fill my two hands with butter. O Mother Yashōda!

pōdumāna veṇṇaiyirundum kaḍaivadēnō tāyē
idu enna vindaiyō māyādēviyin līlaiyē
ulagai kāṭṭiyappin uṇaravillai tāyē
uralōḍu kaṭṭiyiṭṭa anbāna annaiyē
tāyē yaśōdammā

O Mother, why do you keep churning even though there is more than enough butter? How strange! Is it the play of the Goddess of Delusion? Even though I revealed the whole universe to you, you still did not awaken. You even tied me to a mortar, O most loving mother! O Mother Yashōda

gaṇanāyakā devā (Marathi)

gaṇanāyakā dēvā mangaḷamūrtī
śubhadāyaka karī hī prārthanā pūrtī

O Lord Ganesha, You are pure auspiciousness. Please fulfil our prayers, O giver of auspiciousness.

sanmatī dāyaka tū mahāgaṇapatī
sakala guṇāntsāhī tū adhipatī
māgaṇē tuzalā hētsa cintāmaṇī
prēmabhaktī lābhō tuzhiyā caraṇī

You bestow on us a noble mind and noble virtues. O Ganesha, who fulfils all our wishes, please bless us with love and devotion to your feet.

jai gaṇarāyā girījā tanayā
jai gaṇarāyā bāppā mōrayā

Hail Ganesha, son of Goddess Parvati! Lord Ganapati, please bless us!

vighnahara tava kartā japa dhyān
ānandē man lābhē samādhān
māgaṇē tūza hē dīnadayāḷā
sukhaśāntī lābhō sadaiva sakaḷā

O remover of obstacles, when we meditate on you and chant your name, the mind becomes happy and content. O compassionate one, may everyone be happy and peaceful.

gaurīsuta tū varada vināyaka
ōmkārarūpī carācara vyāpaka
māgaṇē āmatsē hētsa prathamēśā
satata bhajāvē tulātsa gaṇēśā

You are the son of Goddess Pārvatī and the giver of boons. You pervade all moving and unmoving beings in the form of the ōmkāra ('Aum' sound). O Ganesha, who is always worshipped first before the start of any endeavour, may we always sing your glories!

gaṇapati bāppā morayā (Marathi)

gaṇapatī bāppā mōrayā he gaṇapatī dēvā
lāḍu mōdak naivēdya premācā svīkārāvā

Father Ganesh please accept this loving offering of Your favorite sweets: laddu, modak.

raktavarṇā śūrpakarṇā rūp tujhē sundar
gajavadanā mūṣaka-vāhanā
gaṇapatī bāppā mōrayā

O Lord of beautiful form, You are reddish in hue and have ever-listening large ears. Rejoice in Father Ganesh, the elephant-faced one, riding on a rat (representing mastery over the senses).

ēkadantā vakratuṇḍā prathama tulā pūjito
lambōdarā ōmkārā gaṇapati bāppā mōrayā

You have a single tusk and a curved trunk. You are always the first to be worshipped. Rejoice in the large-bellied one who is the embodiment of the primal sound Om.

gaṇarāya mangaḷa-dēvā
gaṇapatī bāppā mōrayā gaṇapatī

Victory to Father Ganesh, the auspicious Lord of the Ganas.

bāppā gaṇapatī bāppā
gaṇapatī bāppā mōrayā

Rejoice in our dear Father Ganesh!

vighnaharā sukhakarā gaurīsut vināyakā
sukha-kartā dukh-hartā gaṇapatī bāppā mōrayā

Remover of obstacles, cause of happiness, O Son of Parvati... You give happiness and remove sorrow, victory to You!

bhālacandrā varadahastā jñāna dhana dātā
avināśā matiprakāśā gaṇapatī bāppā mōrayā

You wear the moon on Your forehead, and Your hand is ever-ready to bless us. Victory to the ever-present one who illuminates us with knowledge!

karuṇākarā kṛpāḷā dyāvī nija bhaktī
ādibījā ātmarūpā gaṇapatī bāppā mōrayā

Compassionate Lord please grant me true devotion. I shall rejoice in my Father who is the seed of creation and my true Self

gōvinda gōpāla ani (Telugu)

gōvinda gōpāla ani gānamu sēyarē
śrīkṛṣṇa nāmāmṛta pānamu sēyarē

Constantly chant divine names like 'Govinda' and 'Gopala.' Sip the nectar of Lord Krishna's divine name.

bhāvamu bhakti rasamutō
manasā vācā karmalatō
japamu tapamu kīrtanatō
rāgamu tāḷamu pallavitō

Chant the divine names with ardour and devotion. Worship God in thought, word and deed. Remember Him through japa and tapa (repetition of the divine name and austerities). Praise him through soulful music and meaningful lyrics.

ucchvāsa niśvāsa niṭṭūrpulō
svapna jāgṛti suṣuptilō
ekkaḍiki veḷḷina ēdi cēsina
ekkaḍa uṇḍina ēdi cūsina

Chant the names of the Lord whether inhaling or exhaling, whether dreaming, in deep sleep or awake, wherever you go and whatever you do, wherever you sit or whatever you see.

govinda govinda (Tamil)

govinda govinda govinda govinda
govinda enḍriḍuvōm
viṭhala viṭhala viṭhala viṭhala
viṭhala enḍrum solvōm

We call out to God, Govinda! We also call him Vittala.

kēśava mādhava śrīhari gōvinda
urugi kūppiṭṭāl
dāsanaippōlangu ōḍi vandu avan
paṇindu ninṭriṭuvān

If we call out his names fervently - Keshava, Madhava, Srihari, Govinda - He will come running to us and stand beside us like a humble servant.

uttravar pettravar dēvarum tēṭa
ōḍi oḷindu koḷvān
nāma sankīrttanam kēṭkumiḍam vantu
tānē māṭṭikoḷvān

He will hide when his kith and kin and even the devas search for him. But where there is chanting of his names, he is caught red-handed!

mōhinipōl alankāramum seyta
dēviyayum kavarvān
karuṇayil antapērazhakil avan
dēviyaipōl iruppān

He dresses up like Mohini (Devi), and even Devi gets mesmerized by such beauty. When he dresses up as Mohini he is equal to Devi herself in his beauty and compassion.

kaḷḷattanam piḷḷai kaniyamutan
uḷḷattai koḷḷai koḷvān
bhaktarkaḷin parabhaktiyinai – avan
aḷḷi parukiḍuvān

He steals the hearts of everyone with his childhood pranks. He drinks the ecstatic devotion of the devotees.

gōvinda jaya jaya jaya (namavali)

gōvinda jaya jaya jaya gōpāla jaya jaya jaya
gōvinda jaya jaya jaya gōpāla jaya jaya jaya

Victory to Krishna Govinda, victory to Gopala the divine cowherd.

śrī nandagōpa priyātmaja
balarāmana priyānuja
gōvinda jaya jaya jaya gōpāla jaya jaya jaya
kōṭisūrya samaprabha hṛdivāsa vāsudēva - jaya

Beloved of Nanda and the cowherds, dearest brother of Balarama, victory to Gopala, the divine cowherd! O radiant Lord of my heart, O son of Vasudeva, effulgent like a million suns...

citta cōrana citānanda
naṭanakara nārāyaṇa
gōvinda jaya jaya jaya gōpāla jaya jaya jaya
kōṭisūrya samaprabha hṛdivāsa vāsudēva - jaya

Victory to the stealer of hearts, the divine dancer Narayana. Victory to Govinda. You protect the Vedas and enchant the senses. O radiant Lord of my heart – victory to You!

hṛdayātīl amūlya (Marathi)

hṛdayātīl amūlya ṭhēvā
māgtō tulā punhā punhā
tuzhī bhaktī dēī amhā - āī
tuzhī bhaktī dēī āmhā

I'm asking for the priceless treasure in the heart again and again. O Mother, please give me devotion.

jyās nā kāhī ant nasē kāhī pār
tē prēm māgtō punhā punhā
tuzhī bhaktī dēī āmhā

It has neither end nor boundary. I'm asking for that love again and again. Please give me devotion.

zō asē aḍhaḷ acal
vinayaśīl niścal
tō viśvās māgtō punhā punhā
tuzhī bhaktī dēī āmhā

It is resolute, unwavering, humble and still. I'm asking for that faith again and again. Please give me devotion.

antarīcyā antarāt
hṛdayācyā gābhāryāt
śōdhatō tulā punhā punhā
tuzhī bhaktī dēī āmhā

You are deep within, in the sanctum of the heart. I'm seeking you again and again. Please give me devotion

tuzhe prem dēī āmhā
tuzhī bhaktī dēī āmhā
tuzhā viśvās dēūn āī
rakṣan kar āī

O Mother, please give me love, devotion and faith, and by this protect me.

iruvudu eraḍē (Kannada)

iruvudu eraḍē nōḍu
ī jīvanadalli
iruvudu eraḍē nōḍu
karma māḍu
karmaphala uṇṇu karmaphala uṇṇu

There are just two things in this life: doing actions, and eating the fruits of those actions.

uttama nāḷe bēke? indu
uttama karmava māḍu
manassige bandante māḍi nāḷe
mahādēvanannu dūradiru

Do you want a good tomorrow? Then do good actions today. Don't do what the mind desires today and tomorrow blame the great God.

rāṭṭe tirugisi daṇivāy te? ā
rāṭṭeya kai biṭṭu kūru
manasanu summane kūrisi attā
mahanta tōrida karma māḍu

Are you feeling exhausted turning the wheel? Then keep the wheel aside and sit. Make the mind simply sit in one place, and do as the Guru bids.

baḍavi nānu nī
maḍagidantiruvē
ennuta ūru biḍalu
nī siddhavāgu

'I am but a beggar. I will be as You keep me.' Saying so, be ready to leave the place at any time.

jagamantalō (Telugu)

yo mām paśyati sarvatra sarvam ca mayi paśyati
tasyāham na praṇaśyāmi sa ca me vā praṇaśyati

Whosoever perceives Me (the supreme Self) in all of creation, and all of creation within Me, to him - I am never invisible and to Me such a one is never invisible (Gīta 6.30)

jagamantalō ammanu cūḍu
ammalōnē jagamunu cūḍu
sarva devatalalō ammanu cūḍu
ammalōnē sarva dēvatalanu cūḍu

See the divine Mother in all, see all within the divine Mother. See all gods in the divine Mother, see the divine Mother in every god!

prati aṇuvulō ammanu cūḍu!
andarilōnu ammanu cūḍu
ammalōnē annī cūḍū
viśvamantā vunnadi cūḍū

Perceive the divine Mother in every atom, perceive her in every person. Perceive everything as happening within the divine Mother, perceive the whole universe within her.

dongalō doralō ammanu cūḍu
pēdalō rōgilō ammanu cūḍu
ō manasā ō manasā
ammalōnē sarva mānavulu vunnaru cūḍu

See the divine Mother in the thief, see her in the king. See her in the poor and the sick, O mind, see her alone, in all of humanity.

pakṣulalō ceṭṭlalō ammanu cūḍu
nadulalō koṇḍalalō ammanu cūḍu
ō manasā ō manasā
ammalōnē sarva bhūtamulu
vunnavi cūḍu

See the divine Mother in birds, in trees; see Her in the rivers, in the mountains. See all beings in her alone.

nīlō ammanu cūḍū bāgā cūḍu
ammalōnē nīvu vunnavu cūḍu bāgā cūḍu
vunnadi ammē cūḍū bāgā cūḍu
antā tānē cūḍu bāgā cūḍu
nīvannadi lēdu cūḍu bāgā cūḍu
cūsedi evarō cūḍu bāgā cūḍu
bāgā cūḍu ammanu cūḍu

Look within and perceive the divine Mother therein. Look intently and you will know that you are within the divine Mother. Look! She alone exists. Look deeply, experience that there is no one called 'you'. Perceive the Perceiver, know the Knower, look with alertness, look deep and you will see that there is Mother alone.

janani sakal (Hindi)

jananī sakal jag jananī
bhagat man kumud cāndani nandini
mṛdul śubhad pada yugala
magan dilśaraṇa māngat śankarī

Mother, You alone are the Mother of the Universe. The heart of the devotee is in bliss while gazing at You. My heart longs to take refuge at Your soft auspicious feet, O Mother Shankari.

śaraṇ dāyani śankarī - śiva
hṛday rañjini sundarī
mahiṣa mardini śāmbhavī - sur
bipati hāriṇi vaiṣṇavī

You are Shankari, who gives refuge to the devotees, You have captivated the heart of Lord Shiva. You killed the demon Mahishasura and remove all our obstacles, O Mother Vaishnavi.

jananī jananī jananī jananī jananī jananī jananī
jananī jananī jananī
jananī jananī jananī jananī jananī

O Mother

aruṇ kamal sam vadanī
taruṇ ravi sadṛś śōbhit rūpiṇī
adhar madhur hasi sahita
naṭan tava bhuvana mōhana bhairavī

Your face is like a lovely lotus and Your form is effulgent like the morning sun. Your laughter is extremely sweet, and Your divine dance enchants the world.

janan maraṇ sab haraṇi
amṛtamayi jagat kāraṇi jōginī
kamal bhavan man ramaṇi
dhaval śubh vasan dhāriṇi bhārati

You take us beyond birth and death. O Immortal One, You are the cause of this entire universe, the eternal ascetic. Your lotus eyes captivate my heart; You are adorned in auspicious white, O Bharati!

śaraṇam ambikē śaraṇam ambikē caraṇam
dēvi śaraṇam śaraṇam śaraṇam

O Mother, divine Goddess, we take refuge at Your feet!

jaya jagadīśvarī (Marathi)

jaya jagadīśvarī jaya paramēśvarī
dēī nija sukha prēma
sēvā tava di dhāmā
jaya jagadīśvarī jaya paramēśvarī (2)

Hail to the Mother of the Universe! Grant us love towards You and service to Your feet.

gāna vilōlinī bhakti gītapriya
puravī jana manō kāmanā
gāū mukhī tava nāmā
jaya jagadīśvarī jaya paramēśvarī (2)

Mother, who likes devotional songs and singing, please fulfill my desire: may I sing Your name. Glory to the Mother of the Universe!

śaraṇ mī ālō tava guṇa aikunī
sakala bhakta viśrāmā
dē prēm bhakti āmhā
jaya jagadīśvarī jaya paramēśvarī (2)

I took refuge in You, after hearing about Your divine qualities. You give refuge to all devotees. Grant us love and devotion towards You. Victory to the Mother of the Universe!

sañjīvana sukha sat pada dhāvisī
jāgavī ātmārāmā
param jyōti param dhāmā
jaya jagadīśvarī jaya paramēśvarī (2)

You show us the eternally blissful state, in which God is awakened within. You are the eternal light, the eternal abode. Victory to the Mother of the Universe!

jaya janani caitanya (Telugu)

jaya janani caitanya kusumapriyē
manōpuṣpam arpayāmi

O Divine Mother who loves the offering of Self-awareness, I offer the flower of my mind to you.

nī navvē pūvvulai śānti varṣiñcanī
nī karuṇē mā hṛdilō puṣpiñcanī
jñāna kusumā-lugā vikasiñcanī
suguṇa-mulu sugandha-mai veda-jallanī

May your beautiful smile rain as flowers of peace upon me. May your compassion blossom as flowers in my heart; may these flowers bloom with knowledge and ever emit the fragrance of good qualities.

prēma makaranda-mai niṇḍipōnī
nigraha manu-mullu kāppāḍanī
mṛdubhāva purēkula śōbhalō
hṛdi pūvai pādālu kaḍagani

May these flowers be filled with the honey of love and protected by the thorns of self-restraint. May the beautiful petals of these flowers be soft and gentle. May I wash your lotus feet with such flowers of purity, O Mother!

jhevhā vāṭṭ (Marathi)

jhēvhā vāṭṭ disatu nāhī
uttar gavsat nāhi
āṭṭhav mūrtī viṭṭhōbācī
sād ghāl prēmācī
viṭṭhala viṭṭhala viṭṭhala viṭṭhala jay jay
viṭṭhala pāṇḍuranga
viṭṭhala pāṇḍuranga

When you cannot find a way ahead, and cannot find any answers, remember the beautiful form of Vitthala and call out to him with love. Call to him with the sweet names: 'Vitthala, Panduranga!'

jhēvhā ātu rite bhāsē
kāhi sucēnāse hōtē
sēvā kar tū janāñcī
smarūn prēma viṭṭhāyīce
viṭṭhala viṭṭhala viṭṭhala viṭṭhala jay jay
viṭṭhala pāṇḍuranga
viṭṭhala pāṇḍuranga

When you feel empty within and are not able to think anymore, serve others remembering the love you feel towards Vitthala, and call out 'Vitthala, Panduranga!'

jhevhā sarv sukhē jhālē
kāhi uṇīv nāhi bhāsē
vāts śabda santāṅcē
śōdh kā jagāyajhē
viṭṭhala viṭṭhala viṭṭhala viṭṭhala jay jay
viṭṭhala pāṇḍuranga
viṭṭhala pāṇḍuranga

When everything is going well and nothing is lacking in life read the words of saints and search for the purpose of this life. And remember the sweet names, 'Vitthala, Panduranga!'

pāṇḍuranga pāṇḍuranga pāṇḍuranga

kāḷi karuṇākarī (Tamil)

tāyunnai nāḍivantēn tañcamena tēḍivantēn
intapūvulakam tavikkutammā
bhuvanēśvari nī kāttiḍammā

I have come to You my Mother, searching for refuge in You. This entire Earth is suffering. O Goddess of the world, please protect us.

kāḷi karuṇākarī karumāri bhairavī
āyi mahāmāyi dēvī
vāri vāri aruḷai vazhankum kāḷi bhairavi

O Kali, compassionate one! O Karumari, Bhairavi, Devi, Goddess of Maya! Kali, Bhairavi, you shower endless grace.

caṇḍi cāmuṇḍi caṇḍamuṇḍa marddinī
rudrē bhadrē durgādēvī
ninpāda silambolikka āḍiḍuvāy

O Chandi, Chamundi, You destroyed the demons Chanda and Munda. O Goddess Durga, please dance with Your anklets resounding!

ulakaḷanta uttamanin sōdari
ulakamellām kāttunirkkum nāyaki
paṇivatanai koḍuttu paṇpinaiyum vaḷarttu
manattūymai ākkiḍuvāy dēviyē – atil
karuṇayōḍu kuḍiyiruppāy śaktibhairavī

You are the sister of He who measured the entire universe (Vamana - an avatar of Lord Vishnu), the whole universe is waiting for You. Give me humility, may good qualities dawn within me. O Goddess, primordial energy, be compassionate with me, purify my mind and reside in it.

uyirānāy uravānāy ulakānāy
guṇamānāy kulamānāy tiruvānāy
uruvamāka ānavaḷ aruvamāka ānavaḷ
guruvaḍivāy vazhinaḍattum dēviyē – untan
aruḷai maṭṭum vēṇḍukirōm śaktibhairavī

You are my life, my relative, my world, my character, my family, my Goddess. You are both with form and formless. O Devi, You have taken the form of our guru to guide us, we pray only for Your grace.

bhuvanēśvarī sarvēśvarī paramēśvarī hṛdayēśvarī
aruḷmazhai pozhintiḍuvāy bhairavī
dākṣāyaṇī kātyāyanī māhēśvarī bhavatāriṇī
tiruvaruḷ tantiḍuvāy bhairavī

You are Goddess of the Universe, Goddess of all, Goddess of my heart... O Bhairavi, please shower Your grace! You take us across the ocean of samsara. Please grant Your blessings.

kaṇṇanu naivēdyam (Malayalam)

kaṇṇanu naivēdyam kaṇṇīṛāl-arppiccu
kaṇṇima cimmāte kāttirunnu
innu-varum kaṇṇan innu-varum – ennu
cintayil cittam layiccirunnu... dūre
kālocca kātōrttu kāttirunnu

Having offered my tears as the sacred ritual offering to my Krishna, I now wait ceaselessly, looking out for him with unblinking eyes. All I can think now is that my Krishna will surely come, he will come today... And I wait, expecting to hear the distant sound of his footsteps.

ēkānta sāndramām ātmāvil-utirunna
mahitamām madhurānubhūti-pōle
taḷiriṭum tarunira, itaḷiṭum malarnira
iḷam maññutirunnila-viralukaḷāl – pūkkaḷ
himarēṇu vitarunnitaḷ viralukaḷāl

My longing is like a sweet thrilling feeling arising from the dense loneliness of my soul. It is like dew drops dripping from trees and flowers in a faint light, or like rays of light emerging from scattered dew drops.

yamunayil-ōḷattil sindūram cālikkum
sāyamī sandhyayil manda mandam
arikilēykkārō naṭann-aṇayum pōle
akale ninnoru kālccilambu nādam – kaḷa
madhuramāmoru kālcilambu nādam

As I behold the golden orange flow of the Yamuna river in the setting sun I feel as if someone is approaching me; I hear the sound of your anklets – the sweet sound of your anklets.

taraḷitāmakunnen hṛdayam nin mṛdulamām
karatārin sparśanattālē
ariyanilāvēttu kuḷirunna candana –
taḷirukaḷ tazhukunna pōle – iḷam
taḷirukaḷ tazhukunna pōle

And when my broken heart feels the gentle touch of your hands It is like the caressing touch of the leaves of a fragrant sandalwood tree in the cool moonlight.

kēśava bēgane (Kannada)

kēśava bēgane bā bārō mādhava bēgane bā bārō
nage mukha tōruta yādavanē ōḍi ōḍi bā bārō

Come quickly, Keshava, member of the Yadava race, show me your smile and come running quickly to me!

haṇṇu hampalu savibeṇṇē - ninna
naivēdyakendē tandihenu
taḍavēke prabhuve karuṇeya tōrisi
darśana bhāgyava nīḍemagē

I have brought fruit and butter as offerings for You. O Lord, why do you delay in showing me compassion? Kindly give me your darshan.

śrī nidhi śrī hari kṛṣṇā
jai jai hari hari kṛṣṇā

O Krishna! You are a mine of virtues! Victory to Lord Krishna!

hagalu iruḷu eḍebiḍade - ninna
hāḍuta hogaḷuta nānalidē
maunavētakē gōvindā
tvaritadi bā paramānandā

I sing your praises day and night without cease. O Govinda, why do you remain silent? Giver of supreme bliss, come quickly to me!

divya nāmava japisuta nā - ninna
nirmala prēmava bēḍutihē
śauriyē śaravēgadi bā
śāśvata śaraṇāgati nīḍū

I chant your divine name, seeking only pure love. O courageous one, come flying at arrow-speed, and bestow on me total surrender.

mahāmāyi mahākāḷi (Telugu)

mahāmāyi mahākāḷi mahādēvi sarvamayi

O great Goddess! You are all pervading!

īta rāni pasivāḍinamma
nēnu māyakaḍali dāṭalēnamma
īta nērppi daricērccavamma
nā deggaravuṇḍi dāri cūpavamma

O Mother, this child does not know how to swim. I cannot cross this ocean of delusion. Please help me reach the far shore by teaching me how to swim. Please be by my side and show me the way.

rakṣiñcavamma karuṇiñcavamma

Mother, save me! Be merciful to me!

prārabdhapu alanu dāṭalēnu
nēnu nādanu suḍula īdalēnu
triguṇa makaramula neggalēnu
śakti yuktinicci nērppavamma ītanu

I am unable to overcome the waves of destiny. I am powerless before the whirlpools of 'I' and 'mine.' I am unable to defeat the crocodiles of the three guṇas (natural qualities). O Mother, please bestow on me strength and discernment, and teach me how to swim.

manadinuḷḷil (Tamil)

manadinuḷḷil unnuḍantān nānum pēsuvēn
magizhndirukkum vēḷaitanil unnai koñcuvēn
ekkavalaiyenḍrālum eḍuttu colluvēn
akkaṇattil adutīra amaidi koḷḷuvēn

In my mind, I speak only to you. When I'm happy I fondly play with you. Whatever be my worry I tell you. In an instant, the worry vanishes and I feel peaceful.

annam uṭṭi viḷaiyāḍa poruḍkaḷum tantāy
annaiyunai marandadilē nānum mūzhginēn
āḍikkaḷaittu ammā ena nānum kūvinēn
ādaravāy paḍukka annai maḍiyai tēṭinēn
maḍiyai tēṭinēn

You gave me many worldly amusements to play with. O Mother, I drowned myself in them, forgetting you. When I was tired of playing, I called out 'O Mother!' I searched for you so to lay my head on your lap.

nūru uravu iruntapōdum annaiyāgumō?
noḍippozhudum unai pirindāl vāzhamuḍiyumō?
pūraṇamām un anbil porunta vizhaigirēn
kāraṇankaḷ pārāda karuṇaikkaḍalenḍrō
karuṇaikkaḍalenḍro

Even if there are hundreds of relations, can they be compared to Mother? Is life possible at all if I'm separated from you even for a moment? I have this urge to become One with your pure love. Are you not an ocean of unconditional compassion?

mandahāsavadane (namavali)

mandahāsavadanē tū mandahāsavadanē
mandahāsavadanē tū mandahāsavadanē
varadē varadē
varadē varadē

mandahāsavadanē mandahāsavadanē
mandahāsavadanē mandahāsavadanē

O Mother, whose face beams with an enchanting smile! Please grant me a boon.

himagiri nandini hēmalatē
himagiri nandini hēmalatē

himagiri nandini himagiri nandini
himagiri nandini hēmalatē

Mother, who is the daughter of the ice mountain, who is a golden vine, who is goddess Lalitha...

mantirattirkkilla (Tamil)

mantirattirkkilla īḍu - japam
seytiḍa seytiḍa inikkutu nāvu
ōm namaḥ śivāya enbōm - hara
ōm namaḥ śivāya enbōm

Nothing can be compared to a mantra (sacred name). Repeated chanting of the sacred name gives sweet bliss. Let us chant 'om namah sivaya'.

nīntiḍum jīvan kāṭṭāru
kaḍantiḍalām aḍailkkalamondra uṇḍu
aintezhuttai uccarittu - manamē
eḷitil akkarai ēru

There is only one refuge for us to cross the tremulous ocean of samsara. O mind, chant the five lettered sacred name (namah shivaya) and reach the other shore easily.

ōm namaḥ śivāya enbōm
hara hara śivāya enbōm

Let us chant 'om namah shivaya'

talaividhikaḷ mārum nanku
vinaikaḷil vīriyyam kuraiyum endru
karaikkaṇḍōr sonnatē sollu - manamē
pūraṇa nambikkaikkoṇḍu

This name has the power to change our fate and lessen the negative effects of our karma. O mind, have full faith in the words of those who have already crossed the ocean of samsara, and chant.

manuṣyan-iviḍe (Malayalam)

manuṣyan-iviḍe janiccu bhōgam
koticcu-nēḍunnu
eḍukkuvān-illoḍukkam-onnum
tiriccupōkumbōḷ
taniccu-vannavar taniccu-pōkum tuṇaykkorāḷenyē
kaṇakkeḍuttāl perutta naṣṭam
manuṣya janmaṅgaḷ

Man takes birth and spends his life pursuing different desires, but in the end he returns empty handed. He came alone and he returns alone. Man's life shows a big loss in the final tally book.

vitaccu koytaraniraccu dēham tyajiccu pōkunnu
vitaccu koyyān tiriccu vīṇḍum taniccu pōrunnu
manassu mēniyil bhramiccu mēnmēl
madiccu nīntunnu
urattavṛttikaḷ-alaccutuḷḷum samudra-nirgghōṣam

Man sows and reaps and then abandons the body. He then returns all by himself to sow and reap once more. The mind deludes itself into fulfilling the desires of the body; Man swims maddened in the thunderous ocean waves of endless desires and actions.

manuṣya-jīvitam-uḍaccuvārkkān uṇarttinōvāttān
orikkal-īśvaran-aḍukkal-ettum guru-prabhāvattil
aṇaññu tṛkkazhal vaṇaṅgiyuḷkkaḷam
uṇarnnu-śōbhikke
teliññu sadguru kaṇiññutūkum vijanmasāyūjyam

To remake the life of Man, to awaken him and release him from pain, God will approach in the radiant form of the Guru. When we adore Her divine form, our hearts will awaken and become effulgent. She will compassionately bestow upon us eternal knowledge.

māyē embāḷatā (Kannada)

māyē embāḷatā kaṇiveyelli
biḍugaḍē illā yārigu
sāvina davaṭe indā pārambutillā
duḥkha maḍugeṭṭidē hṛdayāntār-aḷadalli

None can escape from the deep trenches of maya. From the jaws of death there is no escape; misery has crept into the depths of hearts.

sangharṣa manemāḍi sikutilla vimōcanē
kaṣṭagaḷa kaḷedu ānanda triśa nīgisalu
jagadoḷagē ēnnannu huḍuku ttihē
vivēkavā tvaradu konayilladē

Entrenched in conflicts, there is no way to get rid of misery and quench the thirst for happiness. What are you endlessly searching for in the world, discarding your viveka (right understanding)?

ānanda nijasvarūpa vembudu tiḷiyatē
svataha tānu bērē cintanemāḍi
huṭṭu sāvū maddhya naraḷidā
sujñāna dindariyō tatvamasī bōdhanayinda

Without knowing bliss as our own true nature, we mistake ourselves to be individuals; you are caught in the suffering between birth and death. With right knowledge, realize the importance of 'tattvamasi' ('you are That').

mōḍa musukide (Kannada)

mōḍa musukide manavu iḷidide
hūva biriyadalla naguva bīradalla

The clouds have covered the sky, the mind has come down; flowers are not blossoming, neither are smiles spreading.

mōḍa kaṭṭali maḷeya surisali
iḷeya poreyali parjanya
niyama pālisali sṛṣṭi – vidhi
niyama pālisali sṛṣṭi

May the clouds gather, may rain pour down. May rain take care of the Earth; may creation follow its rules.

tapava biḍadiru tavaka biḍadiru
hṛdaya bāgilanu terediḍu
biḍade beḷaguva sūrya – jagava
biḍade beḷaguva sūrya

Do not give up austerities, do not give up longing. Keep the door of your heart open. The sun will surely shine, lighting up the world.

hūva araḷali bēga
hṛdaya varaḷali īga

May flowers blossom soon; may hearts blossom now.

muttamizh-nāyakī (Tamil)

nin pāda malarāka nān māravē ammā
karumāri tañcamaḍaintōm aruḷvāy nī
tērilēri varuvāyē bhuvanamāḷum māṛiyammā

O Mother, please bless me that I may become a flower at your feet. Karumari, we take refuge in you. O Mariyamma, Goddess of the Universe, please come in your chariot.

muttamizh-nāyakī mangaḷa-rūpiṇī
karuṇai-kaḍalē dēvī śaraṇam
paramanin tuṇaiyē umayē satiyē
paramēśvariyē dēvi śaraṇam

Goddess of music, your form is auspicious; ocean of compassion, we take refuge in you. O consort of Lord Shiva, Goddess Uma, O Sati, Supreme Sovereign Goddess, we take refuge in you.

māriyamma śaraṇam –
karumāriyamma śaraṇam
ayimahāmāyi dēvi śaraṇam

Mariyamma, Karumari, Mother, Mahamayi, we take refuge in you!

ōmkāra-nāyakī jyōti-svarūpiṇī
ādiśakti-śūlinī nī śaraṇam
tīcaṭṭiyēntum māntarkku viraivil
tīvinaikaḷ tīrppavaḷē śaraṇam

You are the Goddess of the sacred syllable 'Om', your form is light, You are the primordial power who wields the trident- we take refuge in you. You quickly remove the evil karma of those who come to you with the fire pot (vessel with fire carried on one's head in performance of a vow). We take refuge in you!

maragata rūpiṇī kuyilisai nāyakī
māṇikya cilaiyē śaraṇam
vēppilai ēnti nāḍivarum bhaktarin
kulaviḷakkē tiruviḷakkē śaraṇam

Your beautiful form is like moonstone, and you rule over music. You are of precious form, we take refuge in you. You show the way to the devotees who come with neem leaves, O Goddess, we take refuge in you!

muttu muttu vēlavanē (Tamil)

muttu muttu vēlavanē muttunagai bālakanē
vaṇṇamayil-vāhananē ōḍi vā
muttamizhin kōvalanē sattiyattin kāvalanē
vaḷḷikura-vaḷḷiyuḍan āḍi vā

Lord Muruga, Your form is that of a little boy with a beautiful smile, and you ride a peacock; come running to me. You are Lord of the Tamil language, protector of Truth, come dancing with Valli (consort of Muruga).

vēlavā vaḍivēlavā manamāḍivā mayilērivā
vēlavā vaḍivēlavā tuṇaiyāgavā vinaitīravā

O Muruga, who wields the spear, come dancing on the peacock. O Muruga come save me, rid me of my misfortunes!

ānaiyāga vantu pānaivayiran undan
kādal vaḷḷiyinai turattavē
vēgamāga vandu kāttu kaipiḍitta
vēlan un kathaiyum pāḍinōm
ānaiyāga iṅgu ārupēygaḷ emai
āṭṭivaikkum nilai pārayyā
kākkavēṇḍi iru kaigalkūppi unai
vēṇḍum enkaḷ kurai tīrayyā

We sing the story of when you came quickly to the rescue of your beloved Valli when Lord Ganesh came in the disguise of an elephant and chased her, and thus you were able to take her hand in marriage. Please look at our pitiful state, as we suffer in the clutches of the elephant-like six latent tendencies! With joined palms, we seek refuge in you, that you may rid us of such tendencies.

pārai kalaṅgavaikkum pāvacceyalgaḷ seyda
sūran āṇavattil āḍavē
pāyndu cenḍravanē māyttu nīyum inda
pārai kāttakatai pāḍinōm
pāzhum manadil pala sūrar kuḍiyirundu
āṭṭivaikkum nilai pārayyā
jñānavēl koṇḍu sūravadham seydu
nāḍum enkaḷ kurai tīrayyā

When Suran (the demon) was wallowing in ego and committing sinful acts which made the whole world tremble in fear, you came and protected the world by killing him. We sing these glories you have bestowed on us! Please look at our pitiful state, as our minds are occupied by many such demons (negative tendencies.) Please wield your spear of knowledge and rid us of these negative tendencies.

vēlavā vaḍivēlavā tuṇaiyāgavā vinaitīravā

O Muruga please come save me, rid me of my misfortunes!

nāce tū (Hindi)

nācē tū mama manamē dēvī
cittāmbuj me nācē
dēvī cittāmbuj me nācē
nacēgī jab jananī pyārī

tab sundar sab lāgē
dēvi.tab sundar sab lāgē

Devi You are dancing in my entire being. When my loving Mother is dancing then everything around me is beautiful.

nācē dēvī jagadambē mātē nācē
nācē kāḷīmātē dēvī nācē

Mother Kali please dance!

śyāmē tū is jag kī mayyā
sab antaryāmī tū
śōbhā hai kaṇ kaṇ meṅ tērī
kar mangaḷ kī varṣā
dēvī kar mangaḷ kī varṣā

O Dark One, You are the all-knowing Mother of this Universe. Each and every part of You is extremely enchanting. Please shower auspiciousness on all of us.

dhīm tarikiṭa dhīm tarikiṭa dhīm tarikiṭa dhīm
dhīm tarikiṭa dhīm tarikiṭa dhīm tarikiṭa dhīm

(Sounds of dancing)

tāre sūraj śaśiyē sārē
jag rūpiṇi tū mayyā
mātē mānas sar mēṅ mērē
tava hī mūrtī sōhē
dēvī tava hī mūrtī sōhē

The sun, stars and moon and all. You are the Creatrix of this Universe. O Mother, You preside over my mind and being. O Devi, You alone reside therein.

dēvī mātē jagadambē mātē jaya
dēvī mātē jagadambē mātē
dēvī mā jagadambē mā jaya
dēvī mā jagadambē mā

O Mother of the Universe, Victory to You!

nā eda kōvelalō (Telugu)

nā eda kōvelalō nīrūpuniṇḍanī
nītalapetapasugā nā brattukupaṇḍanī

Let my heart temple be filled with your form. Let your divine form be established in there. Let thoughts of you become my austerity.

kāraḍavi dārilō kārcicu-ragilēnu
ī brattukubāṭṭalō naḍicinēnalasēnu
tōṭunīṭa-yulēni ontari dānanu
dhikkevarikanāku nā cēyivadalaku

A wildfire is blazing in this deep forest of life and I am weary of walking the path. I'm alone without any companions, don't leave my hand, I have no other refuge.

ajñāna-pupenucīkaṭimusirēnu
prārabdhakarmala ūbilō cikkēnu
elugettipilicēnu nātallinīkoraku
ekkekki ēṭu-cēṭṭi pillanu oṭicērcu

I am calling out loudly to you, surrounded by the thick darkness of ignorance, caught in the mire of destiny. Take this child who is crying inconsolably into your lap.

velugunīṭala āṭṭa erukalēdu
mantra tantra pubāṭṭa-nēnaṭavalēdu
nērvagalēdamma-japatapasādhanalu
neranammikoluvani nīpāda padmālu

I do not understand the play of light and shadows; I haven't walked the path of mantra and tantra, I haven't learned to do japa, tapa, sadhana; but I worship your feet with full faith.

nallanivāḍu (Telugu)

nallanivāḍu allarivāḍu cinnikṛṣṇuḍu
muddula kṛṣṇuḍu vāḍu-mōhana-kṛṣṇuḍu

Dark colored, naughty little Krishna. Darling and beautiful Krishna.

venneludōccēḍu madi vennelu dōccēḍu
muvvā-gōpāluḍu-muripāla kṛṣṇuḍu
rēppallē vāsulaku-kannula vennala bāluḍu
gōkula rāyuḍu-manamōhana-kṛṣṇuḍu

He steals butter as well as hearts, He is the little cowherd boy wearing anklets; darling Krishna, light of the eyes of dwellers of Repalle (another name for Gokula), King of Gokula.

kṛṣṇā kṛṣṇā gōpīgōpāla
acyutā śrī bālagōpāla
śrīkṛṣṇā gōvindā manamōhana

Krishna of the gopis, eternal One, cowherd child, Lord Krishna, Lord of the cows, enchanter of the mind!

vēṇuvu-nūdēḍu-manasumai-marapiñcēḍu
vastrālu dōcāḍu-dēhacintanu mārcāḍu
cīralu iccāḍu-draupadi mānam kāccāḍu
līlalu-jēsēḍu-rāsalīlalu āḍēḍu

Playing his flute, he makes everyone ecstatic. He hid away the clothes of gopis to remove body consciousness, but gave sarees to Draupadi to protect her pride. He plays leela (divine play), as well as rasaleela.

nām ek rūp (Hindi)

nām ēk rūp bahu tērē
jyōt ēk anaginat andhērē

You are the One Self that has many forms. One light, with countless darknesses around.

tū hī māyā tū hī kāyā
tūnē hī man kō bhaṭkāyā
dōṣ kisē dūm tumhī batāō
nāṭak ēk pātr bahu tērē

You are illusion, you are the manifestation of forms. You are the one who has distracted my mind. So can You say who is to blame? One drama with a multitude of roles...

tum hī rudan gīt tumhī hō
duśman tum mīt tumhī hō
ghaṭ-ghaṭ kē vāsī mādhav tum
niścit tum sandēh ghane rē

You are sorrow, you are also the music. The enemy is you, and you indeed are the friend. Krishna, you are the One who is everywhere. You are permanent, yet there is the dense darkness of doubts.

tērē gīt tumhī kō arpaṇ
mērā tan man tujhē samarpaṇ
āvāgaman kā bandhan tōḍō
bandhan ēk janm bahu tērē

Your music is offered to you alone. My mind and body are offered unto you. The bond with you is One, yet we are caught in many lives. Cut asunder the cycle of birth and death.

nanda nandanā (Tamil)

nanda nandanā namō nārāyaṇā - nāmam
anudinamum solluvōm
kṛṣṇa gōvinda harē mukundā - nāmam
anudinamum solluvōm

Let us chant daily the divine names of Narayana. Let us chant daily the divine names of Krishna, Govinda, and Mukunda.

lakṣmivilāsā padmanivāsā
sadguṇabhāsā rādhaiyin nēsā
nāmam anudinamum solluvōm - anda
nāmam anudinamum solluvōm
bhavarōga bhayanāśam seydiṭṭa
nāmam anudinamum solluvōm
padabhakti nijamukti tandiṭṭa
nāmam anudinamum solluvōm

You are Lakshmi's consort, You sit on a lotus, and your speech is sweet. You are Radha's beloved. Let us chant that divine name daily. Let us always chant that divine name which destroys the cycle of birth and death. Let us chant that divine name which gives us liberation through total surrender.

dēvakimaindā yaśōdabālā
nandakumārā gōkulapālā
nāmam anudinamum solluvōm – anda
nāmam anudinamum solluvōm
bhavarōga bhayanāśam seydiṭṭa
nāmam anudinamum solluvōm
padabhakti nijamukti tandiṭṭa
nāmam anudinamum solluvōm

Son of Nanda and Devaki, little child of Yashoda, protector of the cowherds! Let us chant that divine name daily. Let us always chant that divine name which destroys the cycle of birth and death. Let us chant that divine name which gives us liberation through total surrender.

bhaktavatsalā śrīparamdhāmā
yādavanāthā mādhavadēvā
nāmam anudinamum solluvōm – anda
nāmam anudinamum solluvōm
bhavarōga bhayanāśam seydiṭṭa
nāmam anudinamum solluvōm
padabhakti nijamukti tandiṭṭa
nāmam anudinamum solluvōm

O Krishna, One who is compassionate to devotees, O Madhava, leader of the Yadava clan. Let us chant that divine name daily. Let us always chant that divine name which destroys the cycle of birth and death. Let us chant that divine name which gives us liberation through total surrender.

vēṇuvilōla vēdavihārā
śōbhanarūpā mōhanahāsā
nāmam anudinamum solluvōm – anda
nāmam anudinamum solluvōm
bhavarōga bhayanāśam seydiṭṭa
nāmam anudinamum solluvōm
padabhakti nijamukti tandiṭṭa
nāmam anudinamum solluvōm

O Krishna, You play the flute, and revel in the Vedas; You have a beautiful form and an enchanting smile. Let us chant that divine name daily. Let us always chant that divine name which destroys the cycle of birth and death. Let us chant that divine name which gives us liberation through total surrender.

nārāyaṇa nārāyaṇa nārāyaṇa
nārāyaṇa nārāyaṇa
nārāyaṇa nārāyaṇa nārāyaṇa
nārāyaṇa nārāyaṇa

nānu nānallavembante (Kannada)

nānu nānallavembante
anantasatyavu tōruttidē
bhāsavāguttidē svayam tānu
prapañcabhrameyu nijavantē
bharisalāgada naṣṭhakke kāraṇa
prapañcabhrameyu nijavantē

The eternal truth that 'I am not I' is dawning upon me. I am beginning to feel that this world is an illusion. I can see the truth that this world of illusion is the cause of endless misery.

arasatā kanasinalli baḍava-nendu
duḥkhisidantē
nammali-mūḍida manōvikārada
grahaṇavu nammannāvarisi
grahaṇavu nammannāvarisi
satyasya satyam brahma ātmai vedam sarvam

Like a king who feels dejected when he has a dream that he is a poor man. The eclipse of our thoughts imprison us in a similar manner. The only truth is the one Self – the supreme atma.

sanātha-ṛṣi iharilli mithyāgrahikeya
tolagisalu
nityasatya tānendu ariyalu
amṛta-tattvabōdhisu tiharu
amṛta-tattvabōdhisu tiharu
satyasya satyam brahma ātmai vedam sarvam

To rid us of this false perception and make us understand the eternal truth, sages of yore ever teach us the immortal principle: the only truth is the Self– the supreme atma.

nijavan ariyadē (Kannada)

nijavan ariyadē nondē nīnu
indrajāla āṭadalli brāntanāgi
vyaktiyalla paramārtthā
samyak jñānadinda nī tiḷi

Without knowing the truth, you are suffering- deluded by the conjuror's play. Individuality is not reality! Know this through right knowledge.

manujā samyak jñānadinda nī tiḷi

O Man, understand reality through right knowledge.

nāma rūpavāgi tōrutiha
sarvātmavanu ariyadeyē
himbālisuvē yēki māyēya
nitya mukta svarūpan ēkkē biḍuvē

You are unable to know the all-pervading atman that is manifest in all the names and forms you behold. Why are you pursuing this illusion? Why are you giving up your ever-free Self?

ēnannu jagadinda bayassiruvē
sukhaduḥkha vemba bhrānti irissī
idēnu mātē divyā nageyē
namissuvē jaganmāteya pāda kamalakkē

What is it that you are expecting from the world? In your delusion you have made fleeting happiness and sorrows your reality. Is this all just the laughter of my divine Mother Kali? I bow down to the lotus feet of the Mother of the Universe.

nijava nariyadē (Telugu version)

nijamu teliyaka nīvu kaṣṭapaḍitivī
indrajāla āṭayandu bhrāntuḍaitivī
vyakti kādu paramārttham
samyak jñānamto telusuko

manujā samyak jñānamto telusuko

nāmarūpamulugā bhāsitamai
caitanyasāram erugakayē
paruguleḍitivi kādā māyavenukā
nityamukta svarūpamunu vadili nīvu

manujā samyak jñānamto telusuko

lēmi ēmani lōkāna vetikēvū
sukha-duḥkhamulu satyamani bhramiñci
ammā idi kaliyoka aṭṭahāsamā – nī
pāda padmamulaku śaraṇamulu

manujā samyak jñānamto telusuko

nīlavaṇṇā (Tamil)

nīlavaṇṇā tāmarakaṇṇā rādhegōvindā
nīṇḍanēram kāttirukkēn rādhegōpālā
kāttukāttu kālgaḷ nōkudu rādhēgōvindā
kāṇādendan uḷḷam vāḍudu rādhēgōpālā

O Radha's Krishna, protector of the cows, Lord Krishna! Your complexion is blue and your eyes resemble lotus flowers. I have been waiting for you for such a long time. I have been standing and looking out for you for so long that my legs are hurting. O Krishna, without a glimpse of you, I start to wilt from within.

mañcaḷvaṇṇa paṭṭukkāra rādhēgōvindā
koñcumozhi pēsiḍuvāy rādhēgōpālā
nañcunīnka endanmīdu rādhēgōvindā
piñcupādam vaittu āḍu rādhēgōpālā
rādhē rādhē rādhē rādhē rādhē gōvindā
rādhēgōvindā rādhēgōpālā

O Krishna, You wear yellow silk, and speak sweet words innocently like a child. Dance with your little feet on me that I may be rid of all the poison (negative tendencies) within.

muttumaṇi mālaittarēn rādhēgōvindā
muttamonnu tandiḍuvāy rādhēgōpālā
pattupāna veṇṇa tarēn rādhēgōvindā
bhaktiyilē pittanākku rādhēgōpālā
rādhē rādhē rādhē rādhē rādhē gōvindā
rādhēgōvindā rādhegōpālā

O Krishna, I will give you a pearl necklace; please give me a kiss, Radhe Gopala! I will give you a pot of butter... Please make me intoxicated in your devotion.

rādhē rādhē rādhē rādhē rādhē gōvindā
rādhē rādhē rādhē rādhē rādhē gōpālā
mādhavā manamōhanā yādavā yadunandanā

O Madhava, enchanter of my mind, O Yadava, son of Yadu.

oru nalil ñan (Tamil)

oru nāḷil nāṇ en kaṇṇanai kāṇbēn
oru gāna tēnisai kēṭpēn
sevvidazhkaḷilē vēnkuzhal patittu
cella kaṇṇan en munvaruvān

anṭrendan piravi payan peruvēn
anṭru nān ānanda padam aṭaivēn
unmatta bhaktiyin uyarkoṭumuṭiyil
ninṭru nān ānanda naṭam purivēn

jīvarāśikaṭkellām ādhāramāy nirkkum
īśvaran nī pārin kāvalanē
kaṇamum tāmadam ini vēṇḍām
īśvarā unai nān kaṇḍiṭavē

oru nimisham (Tamil)

oru nimiḍamāvadu amaidi uṇḍō
ulakiyal sukham tēṭi alaiyum manidā
unakkoru nimiḍamāvadu amaidi uṇḍō

paramārtta tatvankaḷ ariyāmal māyaiyin
nizhaladan pinnē mayanki ōdi
erikinḍra tīkkaṇḍu vishukinḍra viṭṭilāy
oru palanum illādoṭunka toḍankināy

kṛmiyāy puzhuvāy izhaikinḍra uyirinam
palavāgi paravaikaḷ vilankumāgi
sīrāga uyarnduyarntātmānubhūtiyin
mānita piraviyāl payan ennavō

adarkkalla manidanin aridānadām piravi
adarkkuṇḍu laṭciyam adanai vēṇḍi
nān enadu enkinḍra mayakkam teḷindu nī
hari hara parabrahma bhajanai seyyādinku

pañcēndriya (Kannada)

pañcēndriya nilissī pañcākṣari japissī
karedare baruvanu ennu namma śivanū

Bringing to a halt our indulgence in the five senses, if we chant the five syllabled mantra (namah shivaya) and call out to Him, our Shiva will come to us.

śambhō mahādēva śambhō
śāmbhavīdēva śambhō
haraśambhō śivaśambhō
śivaśambhō hara śambhō
śambhō mahādēva śambhō

O auspicious great Lord Shiva!

pāvanarūpa śambhō
pāpanivāraka śambhō - banni
nāmajapissuva madduśivanā
pālayamām śambhō

Lord Shiva's form is pure and he is the destroyer of sin. Come let us chant the name of the sweet Lord; protect us, O Shambho!

triśūladhāri śambhō
trinētradhārī śambhō
trikkaiyallī harassu śambhō
trikālajñāni śambhō

O Shiva, You bear the trident and have three eyes. – bearer of the Trishula, Bless us, O Lord of supreme knowledge.

paripāvana (Marathi)

paripāvana caritē sundara vadanē
caraṇī karitō naman
ambā dēśīl kadhī darśan

O Mother, you have a pure story and a beautiful face. You uplift the downtrodden. I bow down to your feet. When will you grant your darshan?

durgē tū lakṣmī tuḷjā bhavānī
kitī rūpē kitī nāmē tujhē ambē
pari tēj ēkac prēmācē

You are Durga, Lakshmi and Tulja Bhavani. How many names and forms you have! Each of these forms bear the same splendor of love.

ātmajñānācē vardān dē
sāyujy saukhyācē dān tū dē
tava caraṇāñci bhakti tū dē

Give us the boon of self-realization, liberation and devotion to your feet.

jay jagadambē ā-ī bhavānī
bhavatāriṇī tū mātē

Hail to the Mother of the Universe, O Mother Bhavani! You take us across the ocean of samsara.

premasandāyini (Marathi)

prēmasandāyinī bhaktipradāyinī
dayāmayī ambā jagadōddhāriṇī

O Mother, You awaken love and give devotion; You are the compassionate one who uplifts the world.

śaktirūpī ambā vyāpī carācarī
anantbhāv tav sṛṣṭicakr phirī
karmabhaktī jñān de sakalā uddharī
prēmasandāyinī jagadōdhāriṇī

O Mother, you pervade all creation in the form of primal energy, your infinite forms sustain this creation. O Mother, who awakens love and uplifts everyone, please give right knowledge, devotion and action, and uplift all.

satkāry ghaḍū de nirantar sevā
kāyā vācā manī arpūni bhāva
hīc kharī sādhanā sukṛtātcā ṭhevā
bhaktipradāyinī jagadōddhāriṇī

May we always do righteous actions and service by offering our devotion in the form of words, thoughts and deeds. This alone will be real sadhana (austerities), and endowment of good karma. O Mother, you give devotion and uplift everyone.

tav smaraṇe manī guṇgān gāyī
sadā antarangi anubhūtī yē-ī
jīvan sārth jhāle līn tav ṭhāyī
dayāmayī ambā jagadōddhāriṇī

I sing your glories remembering you, and experience your presence within. My life has been fulfilled by surrendering to you, O compassionate Mother who uplifts everyone.

udē-g ambē udē-g ambē udē-g ambē ā-ī

Hail to Mother!

prēmasūrya (Kannada)

prēmasūrya nīnu udisi bandeyā
bimmanendu lōkabeḷagu tiruveyā
manadimōḍa kavidu enage kāṇadāgide
ninna vaibhava ninna pūrṇṇaprabhe

O Sun of divine love! Have you risen? Are you shining on the world? Clouds have gathered in my mind, I cannot see your glory or your grandeur in full.

ninna beḷakkinallē lōkabeḷagīde
nissargavellā ninna bhavyaniyamave
mōḍavemba līlayū ninna sṛṣṭiye
bēḍutiruve tōribā jñāna-sūryane

The world runs by your light alone. All of nature abides by your regulation. The play of clouds is also part of your creation. O Sun of knowledge, I beg of you: please make yourself visible that I may see you.

andheyalla nānu ninna kāṇabayassūve
manadamōḍa sarissuguruve kṛpetōru nī
antaranga hogalī ninna prēmakiraṇa
hṛdayavaraḷī āgalenna janmapāvana

I am not blind. I long to see you. O Guru, show mercy and draw away the clouds from my mind. May your rays of love enter within me, may my heart blossom, and by this my life will be fulfilled.

puṇḍalika varadā (Marathi)

puṇḍalika varadā karuṇākarā
śrīharī ubhā bhīmā tīrā
nārāyaṇa harī pāṇḍurangā
viṭṭhala viṭṭhala śrīpāṇḍurangā

Hari is standing on the banks of the river Bhima; He is the compassionate one who bestowed his blessings on Pundalika. Lose yourself in the sweet names of the Lord – Narayana, Vitthala, Panduranga!

dēvakī nandana prēmasindhō
ānāth-nāthā dīnabandhō
nārāyaṇa harī pāṇḍurangā
viṭṭhala viṭṭhala śrīpāṇḍurangā

The son of Devaki is an ocean of love, refuge to the helpless and relative of those in need. Lose yourself in the sweet names of the Lord – Narayana, Vitthala, Panduranga!

bhaktavatsalā paṇḍarināthā
smaraṇa mātrē harē bhavacintā
nārāyaṇa harī pāṇḍurangā
viṭṭhala viṭṭhala śrīpāṇḍurangā

Vitthala, Lord of Pandharpura, is full of love for the devotees. The very thought of Vitthala removes all our worries. Lose yourself in the sweet names of the Lord – Narayana, Vitthala, Panduranga!

dīnadayāḷā kṛṣṇagōpāḷā
kaivalyadhāmā bhakta pratipāḷā
nārāyaṇa hari pāṇḍurangā
viṭṭhala viṭṭhala śrīpāṇḍurangā

He is Krishna, the cowherd- compassionate towards the downtrodden. He cares for devotees and takes them to liberation. Lose yourself in the sweet names of the Lord – Narayana, Vitthala, Panduranga!

parabrahma anādi anantā
pāṇḍuranga harī rakhumāī nāthā
nārāyaṇa harī pāṇḍurangā
viṭṭhala viṭṭhala śrīpāṇḍurangā

The Lord of Rukmini, Panduranga, is without beginning or end- He is the supreme Brahma. Lose yourself in the sweet names of the Lord – Narayana, Vitthala, Panduranga

viṭṭhala viṭṭhala pāṇḍurangā
jay jay viṭṭhala pāṇḍurangā
viṭṭhala viṭṭhala pāṇḍurangā
jay jay viṭṭhala pāṇḍurangā
viṭṭhala viṭṭhala viṭṭhala viṭṭhala
viṭṭhala viṭṭhala viṭṭhala viṭṭhala

May You ever be victorious, Lord Vitthala Panduranga!

rāga vairikaḷ (Telugu translation)

rāga dvēṣamu tolaganī
duḥkhātiśayamū śamincanī
mānasam bhava śōka tāriṇī
ammalō vilīnamai

pāpa pūrita chāyalantamai
tattvamu dṛḍhamavvanī
chinmayī nī darśanam tō
chitta bhramalū aṇaganī

manō vyadhalū antamavvanī
bhēda bhāvam naśincanī
dhanyamavvanī ī nā janmamu
man manō sukha kāriṇi

tāpanāśini nī madhūsmitam
nannu anughrahincanī
āśāpāśamulannī tunci - nī
śānti dhāmamu cērani

rāmā jaya jaya rāmā (namavali)

rāmā jaya jaya rāmā
japisuvē rāmā mangaḷa nāmā
rāma rāma jaya jaya rāmā

Victory to Lord Rama! Chant his auspicious name!

śaraṇāgata jana paripālā
vaidēhi arppita mālā
pūrita vividha līlā jālā
rakkasarigē nī kālā

He protects those who have surrendered to him. Sita chose him as her consort by garlanding him. He enacted many a divine sport. He dispatched demons!

rāmā jaya jaya rāmā

Victory to Lord Rama!

daśaratha suta jagadōddhārā
sītā vallabha vānara sēvyā
lakṣmaṇāgrajā lavakuśa janakā
rakṣisu namma anavaratā

Son of Dasharatha, Lord Rama uplifts the world. Rama, the consort of Sita, was served by the monkeys. He was brother to Lakshmana, and father of Lava and Kusha. O Rama, please watch over us constantly.

dīnōddhāraka dharma pālakā
durita nivāraka bhavabhaya hāraka
karuṇārasa śāśvata sukhadāyaka
prēma bhakti mōkṣa pradāyaka

Savior of the fallen and protector of righteousness, he puts an end to misery and dispels both fear and transmigration. Essence of compassion, giver of eternal happiness, he bestows pure love, devotion and liberation!

sādi tōjāle (Tulu)

sādi tōjāle satyōdu sādi tōjāle
nemmadida sukha badukugu sādi tōjāle
ātmaśakti korulemma kaṣṭolen sahisare
paramapāvane dēvi namaku īrē āsare

Show me the way to the truth, show me the way to a peaceful, happy life. O Mother, give me the self-confidence to bear sorrows. O most pure Devi, you are our only refuge.

nanala bōḍu nanala bōḍu namaku panpi āselu
dūramaltuṇḍu manaḥ-śanti samādhāno
svārtha buddhi uppunaga pōparīr dūranē
divya jñāna bhakti kordu kāpulemma bēgane

So many hidden desires torment us, snatching away our peace of mind. Our self-centered mind is ever taking us far away. Give us divine knowledge and devotion and save us O Mother!

paramēśvari dēvi ambikē mahāmāyē (2)

Supreme Goddess, Mother, great illusion!

jīvanada duḥkhōlegu manassonje kāraṇa
satsanga kīrttaneḍe untālemma manassunu
ātma yān śarīro attu panpi bōdha korppadu
dāṭṭalemma bhava-sāgara dēvi karuṇāmayi

The fickle mind is the sole reason for the sorrows of life. Bless us that through satsang and kirtan our minds may be purified. By this we will be able to uplift ourselves through right knowledge. Help us cross this ocean of transmigration (cycle of birth and death), O compassionate Goddess!

śēṣaśayana (Kannada)

śēṣaśayana kamala nayanē
śrīnivāsa śrīdayānidhē
śrīdharā mukunda mādhavā – harē
madhur vadana madhusūdanā

Compassionate lotus-eyed Lord Srinivasa, reclining on the serpent Shesha... You are the auspicious giver of liberation, the Lord of beautiful form, destroyer of evil.

hagalu iraḷuninnabhajisi he
japatapānuṣṭhāna gaidihe
kṛpādṛṣṭi bhīralārēyā
muddu mukhava tōralārēyā

Day and night I sing Your glories. Chanting your name and worshipping you. Will you not cast on me your compassionate glance? Will you not reveal your sweet, loving face to me?

nanda nandanā ānanda mōhanā

Enchanting son of Nanda, Lord of supreme bliss!

ninna kāṇuvāsē mūḍidē
nīnē āśrayā kṛpānidhē
bhaktavatsalā nīnallavē
dīna bandhu birudu ninnadē

The desire to behold you has arisen. You are my only refuge, compassionate one. Aren't you the one that showers love on his devotees? Aren't you the one with the title of 'friend of the poor'?

janma pāvanakkē āśisi
ihada saukhyavannu tyajisihē
ninnapāra karuṇē illadē
nānu ēnu alla tiḷidihē

Wanting to purify this life, I renounced the pleasures of this world. Finally I have realized that without your infinite compassion I am indeed nothing.

nanda nanda nandanā ānanda candana
nanda nanda nandanā ānanda mohana

Enchanting son of Nanda, Lord of supreme bliss!

sirikka connāḷ (Tamil)

sirikka connāḷ – nammai
sirikka connāḷ
nam ammā nammai sirikka connāḷ

Mother told us to laugh, our Mother told us to laugh.

pirandadu mudalē pōgira varaikkum
sirippadai marandu azhudu koṇḍirukkum
ariviliyai eṇṇi sirikka connāḷ - anda
ariviliyai eṇṇi sirikka connāḷ
iruppadai koṇḍu magizhvadai marandu
parappadai eṇṇi varuttattil vāḍum
pēdaiyinai eṇṇi sirikka connāḷ - anda
pēdaiyinai eṇṇi sirikka connāḷ

We have forgotten how to laugh. We cry from the moment we are born and until we leave this world. Mother told us to laugh looking at this ignorance. People forget to be happy with what they have and they struggle in sorrow thinking about what they cannot have. Mother told us to laugh at such ignorance.

dinam dinam palarum irappadai kaṇḍum
tān maṭṭum nilaikka pōvadāy eṇṇum
maḍamaiyinai kaṇḍu sirikka connāḷ - anda
maḍamaiyinai kaṇḍu sirikka connāḷ
aḍuttoru śvāsamum illai nam kaiyyil
arindum poruḷai tanakkena sērkkum
arpapadarai kaṇḍu sirikka connāḷ - anda
arpapadarai kaṇḍu sirikka connāḷ
Even though we see many people dying all the
time we think that we are immortal.

Even though we see many people dying all the time we think that we are immortal. Mother told us to laugh at such ignorance. Even after knowing that the next breath is not in our hands, people keep accumulating wealth. Mother told us to laugh at such ignorance.

vidhiyinai kaṇḍu sirikka connāḷ – vellum
madiyinai koṇḍu sirikka connāḷ
sadiyinai kaṇḍu sirikka connāḷ – tannai
gatiyāy koṇḍu sirikka connāḷ
galagalanenḍru sirikka connāḷ
kavalaiyai marantu sirikka connāḷ
kaikaḷai koṭṭi sirikka connāḷ - anda
kālanai venḍru sirikka connāḷ

Mother told us to laugh at fate by using our intellect which can overcome it. Mother told us to laugh at the crookedness by taking Her as our sole refuge. Mother told us laugh loudly forgetting all our worries. Mother told us to clap our hands and laugh. She told us to laugh, gaining victory over the lord of death .

sirikka connāḷ (Marathi version)

ānandsvarūpī tumī ānandī rahā
ambā sāṅgē ānandi rahā

Bliss is your true nature, be blissful. The divine Mother is ever with you, be blissful.

ānandānē tumhī sārē hasā rē
itarān nāhi tumhī ānand dyā rē
phulvā hāsya tumhī ānandī rahā
ambā sāṅgē ānandī rahā
havē nakō mhaṇat śōdhat rāhilā
dēvāne dilē dē visarūn gēlā
sānḍūnī śōdh ānandī rahā
ambā sāṅgē ānandī rahā

Looking beyond yourself, give happiness to others. Laugh fully, be joyful and dwell in happiness with the divine Mother. Ever lost in likes and dislikes, you have forgotten the blessings the Lord has bestowed.

ānandācē kṣaṇ rē yē-ūn gēlē
man tujhē bhūtbhaviṣyāt ramlē
vartamānī tumhī jagaṇē śikā
ambā sāṅgē ānandī rahā
sthān mān dhan māyēcā pasārā
khēḷ cāle hā niyatitsā sārā
śāntī miḷe nissaṅg hōtā
ambā sāṅgē ānandī rahā

Stop brooding over the past and worrying about the future. Be in the present and dwell in joy with the divine Mother. You are ensnared by the illusion of name, fame and wealth; realize that this is the play of maya, that traps us in the cycle of karma. Detachment from worldly desires brings peace. Dwell in joy with the divine Mother!

ā-ī jagadambā javaḷ āhē
premānē bhaktāñcī vāṭ pāhē
arpūni karm alipt rahā
ambā sāṅgē ānandī rahā
prēm svarūpī tumhī ānandī rahā
cinmayarūpī tumhī ānandī rahā
amṛtasvarūpī tumhī ānandī rahā
ānandarūpī tumhī ānandī rahā

Come close to the divine Mother, the way to love and devotion will open up before you. Surrendering all deeds to her, stay detached and dwell with her in joy. You are the embodiment of love and knowledge, dwell in joy. You are the embodiment of immortality and bliss, dwell in joy.

śivanenīnu (Kannada)

śivanenīnu ellavannu nōḍutiruve
mukkaṇṇa ellavannū kāṇutiruve
dhyānadalli līnavāgi jagava nōḍuve
kaṇṇugaḷa muccikoṇḍe karuṇe tōruve

O Shiva, you perceive everything. O three-eyed One, you see everything. you see the world, even though you are absorbed in meditation. Your eyes are closed, yet you still show compassion.

viśvarūpa divyarūpa lingarūpane
amṛtamūrttidivyajyōti jñānadīpave

Universal, divine form of Shivalinga! Immortal form, divine light, light of knowledge.

nandininna dhyānadalli magnaniruvanu
kaṇṇuteredu ninnanne nōḍutiruvanu
mayyellā kaṇṇāgi tapisuttiruvanu
sēvegāgi sannaddha nirata niruvanu

The holy bull Nandi is absorbed in meditation on your form. With eyes open he is meditating on you. He is performing austerities, as if he has eyes all over his body. He is ever ready to jump into action in order to serve you.

vṛṣabhadēvā bhṛngimitrā śivana vāhanā
raytabandhu hullu mēvā muddu basavaṇṇā

O bull-god, you are the friend of Bhringi (one of Shiva's companions), you are Shiva's vehicle. You are the friend of the farmer, you eat grass, you are beloved Basavanna (local name for the bull).

dēvaśivane – jīvanandiye
guruveśivane – śiṣyanandiye
tāyiśivane – śiśuvunandiye

Shiva, You are God, Nandi the individual soul. You are Guru, Nandi disciple. You are Mother, Nandi infant...

śiva śiva rudra śivā (Telugu)

śiva śiva śiva śiva śiva śiva rudra śivā

śiva śiva śiva śiva śiva śiva rudra śivā
śiva śiva śiva śiva śiva śiva rudra śivā

tṛkāgnikālāya kālāgni rudrāya
nīlakaṇṭhāya mṛtyuñjayāya
namo namaḥ namo namaḥ
namo namaḥ namo namaḥ
tṛkāgnikālāya kālāgni rudrāya
nīlakaṇṭhāya mṛtyuñjayāya
namo namaḥ namo namaḥ
namo namaḥ namo namaḥ

Shiva, you are the blue-throated Lord who is beyond death, our prostrations to you. With the fire of your meditation, you are beyond time. Our prostrations to you.

poyyilōni nīppu nīvē śiva
illunikālce maṇṭa nīvē śiva
paṇṭalu paṇḍince varṣamu nīvē
pairunu muncē varadā nīvē

paṇṭalu paṇḍince varṣamu nīvē
pairunu muncē varadā nīvē

It is your energy that becomes the fire that cooks food. It is also your energy that becomes the fire that causes destruction. You are the rain that brings bounteous harvests, and you are also the rain that causes destructive floods.

śiva-śiva śiva-śiva śiva-śiva śiva-śiva
śatruvu lōni mitruḍu nīvē
mitruḍu lōni śatruvu nīvē
ghōramaghōramu nīvē śiva
nī śikṣa rakṣamāgu śivamē śiva
ghōramaghōramu nīvē śiva
nī śikṣa rakṣamāgu śivamē śiva

You are the friend in the form of an enemy, and also the enemy in the form of a friend. Auspiciousness and inauspiciousness - both are aspects of you. Protection s from you, adversity is also from you. You use both of these to show your child the way to freedom.

śiva-śiva śiva-śiva śiva-śiva śiva-śiva

Some say love (English)

Some say love is just a word: that's only heard

Some search for love
It can't be found, though it's all around

Some say love is lost
Some buy love at any cost

Some die for love
Hoping it's high above

Some cry love is pain
Some call love just a name

Love is our true Self
Love is our only wealth

My Mother's love is everywhere
She will take you there

Ma Om Om Ma

śrī rāma rāma rāmetī (Marathi)

śrī rāma rāma rāmētī, rame rāme manōramē
sahasranāma tattulyam rāma nāma varāṇanē

Chanting the name of Sri Rama just three times is equivalent to reciting the entire list of the Lord's thousand names.

bōla rām rām rām rām rām rām rām

Chant Ram Ram Ram...

rām nām tzapā sadā
rām nām smarā sadā
tzapāne paramāvasthā tū sādh rē

Chant the name of Rama forever. Remember the name of Rama forever. Attain the ultimate state chanting his name.

rām nām japā ithē
rām nām japā tithē
samaj rē paramāvasthā kālātīt rē

Chant the name of Rama here. Chant the name of Rama there. Understand that the ultimate state is beyond space.

bōla rām rām rām rām rām rām rām rām
rām rām rām rām rāmā
rām rām rām rām rāmā
rām rām rām rām rāmā rām
bōla rām rām rām rām rām rām rām rām

rām nām japā ātā
rām nām japā nantar
samaj rē paramāvasthā sthalātīt rē

Chant the name of Rama now. Chant the name of Rama later. Understand that the ultimate state is beyond time.

śrīvāri pādālu (Telugu)

śrīvāri pādālu śirasā namāmi
śrīhari nāmālu hṛdaye smarāmi
śrīhari śrīhari śrīhari anavōy
śrīhari śrīhari śrīhari anavōy

I bow down and touch my head to the feet of Lord Sri Hari. I chant in my heart the names of the divine Lord. Chant Sri Hari, Sri Hari!

ādimūlamitaḍu anni jīvulaku
vēdasvarūpuḍī vēnkaṭēśvaruḍu
gōvulakāparī gōvinduḍēnu
gōvuvai mora etti ārtitō piluvu

He is the primal cause of all beings. He is Lord Venkateshvara, embodiment of the Vedas. He is Govinda the divine cowherd. Call out to him like a calf frantically calling out to its mother...

vēdamulē śilalaina vemkanna girulu
vēdana hariyimcu vēnkaṭa nāmamu
ēḍukomḍala-vāḍā! ēmi ivvagalamu?
pāḍu-kondumu nīdu pāṭalu nityamu

The Vedas have become the seven hills on which the Lord resides (holy place of Tirupati). Chanting his name, our sorrows vanish. Lord of the seven hills – what can I give you? All I can do is constantly sing your glories.

gata janma karmala khātālu mānpi
satatammu nī nāma smaraṇamu immu
kṣaṇa vīkṣaṇamu cālu lakṣaṇamugānu
manalōni pāpālu maṭumāyamagunu

Please close the account of the deeds from previous lives, and grant me the boon that I may incessantly chant your name. A single glimpse of the Lord has the power to vanquish the sins of lifetimes.

pāhi parātparuḍā! vēnkaṭa nāyakuḍā!
pāpa vināśakuḍā! tirumala pālakuḍā!

Lord Venkata Nayaka is the refuge of all, the destroyer of sins, O Lord of Tirumala!

tāḷ paṇintōm (Tamil)

tāḷ paṇintōm tāḷ paṇintōm tankamuttumārī
vēdanayai pōkkiḍuvāy vēppilaikkāri
kāṇavantōm kāṇavantōm kāḷi mahāmāyi
kāṇpatellām unnuruvē kaṇkaḷ vēṇḍum kōḍi

O Muttumari, You hold neem leaves, we bow down at your feet, please remove our sorrows. O Kali, Mahamayi (Goddess who creates illusion), we have come to see you, please give us a million eyes to see everything which is nothing but your form.

ālakāla viṣamuṇḍa ādiśivanmēni
aravaṇaittu kāttiḍum em annaikoṇḍāḷ pāti
pāraṇaittum pātukākkum pārvatiyum nīyē
āḷavantāy āḷavantāy ārumukhan tāyē

You are our Mother who embraces and protects us, and you occupy half of Shiva's body – He who consumed the deadly poison. You protect the entire Universe as Goddess Parvati. O Mother of Lord Muruga, you have come to rule us.

sintanayil vantiḍuvāy selvamuttumārī
santatamum sentamizhil pāḍivantōm dēvī
anparkaḷai āṭkoṇḍiḍum ammā śivaśakti
nāḍivarum bhaktarnalam kākkum abhirāmi

O Muttumari, please reside in our thoughts. O Goddess, we shall always come to you singing your praises in pure Tamil. O Mother, you are the union of Shiva-Shakti, you take your devotees into your fold. O Abhirami, you protect those who take refuge in you.

tāyillā piḷḷayō (Tamil)

tāyillā piḷḷayō nān
nīyillayō enakku?
pārammā un makanin paritavippai
yārammā gati enakku?

Am I a child without a mother? Are you not there for me? O Mother please see your child's suffering.. who else is there as my refuge?

āyiram mukhankaḷ-iḍaiyil – nān
annai mukham tēḍinēn
anbozhukum mozhikaḷ iḍaiyil – nān
ātmārta mozhi vizhaindēn

I searched for my Mother's face amidst a thousand faces. I yearned for soulful words amidst so many (superficial) loving words.

āyiram uravu vandālum – adu
annaikku īḍiṇaiyāmō?
aravaṇaikkum un kaikaḷināl en
ārāda tuyar nīnkumō?

Even if there may be a thousand relationships, will any be equal to Mother? Will my unhealing sorrow be removed by your embrace?

tiruvaḍi pukazhppāḍa (Tamil)

tiruvaḍi pukazhppāḍa varam tā ammā
dinamunnai manamnāḍa aruḷvāy ammā

O Mother, please grant me the boon that I may be able to sing the glories of your divine feet. O Mother, please bless me that my mind may always seek you.

aṇaiykkum nin abhayakkarankaḷ
karuṇai migunda nayanankaḷ
bhaktarai īrkkum un azhakum - ammā
ānandattēnssuvai un bhāvam
ānandattēnssuvai un bhāvam

Your hands embrace and provide refuge to us. Your eyes brim with compassion. O Mother, your beauty attracts your devotees. Your divine moods are blissfully sweet like honey.

oppillā oḷiviḷakkē nī
omkāra tiruviḷakkum nī
māṇikkya maṇiviḷakkum nī
mangaḷankaḷ aruḷum viḷakkē
mangaḷankaḷ aruḷum viḷakkē

You are the incomparable light. Your are the divine light of the sound 'Om'. You are the light of precious gems. You are the light that bestows all auspiciousness.

vāzhkaiyoru (Tamil)

vāzhkaiyoru nīṇḍadūra payaṇam sāmbaśivanē
vazhiyainangu amaittukoḷḷa vēṇum sadāśivanē
cinnadoru punnagaiyum nalla nālu vākkugaḷum
seydiḍumē arppudankaḷ sorggamākkum
bhūmiyaiyum

O Samba Shiva, life is like embarking on a very long journey; please help us to pave the path well. A little smile and a few kind words can work wonders and make this Earth a heaven.

tanakku enna vēṇḍumenḍru
manadu sollittarumō - adu
aṭuttavarkkum vēṇḍumenḍru arivu sollittaraṇum
kaṇakku pārttu varuvatuṇḍō
naṭpum nalla uravum nalla
idayampārttu varuvadilē iruppatuṇḍō pirivum ō
śivanē aruḷvāy haranē

The mind keeps desiring things for itself, but the intellect should teach that others also want similar things. Good friends and relations don't come to us with a calculating mind. When relationships are connected through the heart, there is no question of separation. O Shiva, Hara, please bless us!

maraṇadēvan payaṇamadan irudiyilē varuvān
manam naḍunka kayiradanai urudiyoḍu erivān
mārkkaṇḍēyan pōla anda śivanaḍiyai paṇindāl
maraṇamilā peruvāzhvin arivadanai aruḷvān
ō śivanē aruḷvāy haranē

The Lord of Death will come to meet us at the end of the journey. He will firmly throw his noose on us, making our hearts tremble. Like Markandeya (the 16-year old boy who was saved and made immortal), if we hold onto Lord Shiva's feet, he will bless us with knowledge; we will thus achieve a life of immortal bliss. O Shiva, Hara, please bless us!

śiva śiva śiva śiva śiva śiva śankarā
hara hara hara hara hara hara śankarā
śiva śiva śiva śankarā
hara hara hara śankarā

vinavite (Marathi)

vinavitē bālakṛṣṇā manamōhana vanamālī
madhur bāsurī surānē tū
madhur bāsurī surāne sād malā ghālī
sād malā ghālī sād malā ghālī

I pray to you little Krishna, who captures the mind and is adorned with garlands of wild flowers. Please call me to you by playing sweet music on your flute.

vṛndāvanī jāsī tū gōdhan cārāyā
muralī nādāne vallarī harṣāyā
āsamant sārē pulakit hōṇyā
hēc sūr bāsarīcē maj mōhavī

You go to Vrindavan to graze cows, and to fill the forest with melodies from your flute. That flute sound, which makes all the surroundings light up, entices me.

kuñjavanī gōpāl savaṅgaḍī jamavunī
sarvānmukhī kālā ghās bharavūnī
bhagavant rūp pari jāsī misaḷūnī
hēcī rūp sukhavī mājhyā nayanī

In the forest, O cowherd boy, you gather all your friends and feed them kala (a dish that Krishna used to prepare by mixing all dishes that everyone brings). That sight fills me with joy.

sakhī rādhārāṇī gōpikāñcyā ghēryāt
rāsalīlā karunī vasē sarva hṛdayāt
sarvānsange rangūnī ēkatva antarāt
bhēṭē asācī mājhyā vyākuḷ manī

Along with Radha, all the gopis surround you. You dance with them and dwell in their heart. You play with everyone, seeing One within. I have an intense longing to meet you.

rādhākṛṣṇā rādhikaramaṇā rāsavihāri kṛṣṇā
gōkulabālā gōpīkāntā kuñjavihāri kṛṣṇā
kuñjavihāri kṛṣṇā
rādhē kṛṣṇā rādhē kṛṣṇā
kṛṣṇā rādhe kṛṣṇā

yellā daiva ondē (Kannada)

yellā daiva ondē manujā yellā daiva ondē
adondē iruva śāśvata caitanya śaktiyū
rāmā annu kṛṣṇā annu śivā annu śivē annu

O Man, all deities are but different expressions of the one divine consciousness. That power is the only force that prevails eternally in the universe. We might call that power 'Rāma,' 'Sītā,' 'Shiva' or 'Shivē' ('Shakti'). Regardless, there is only one divine consciousness.

sītā rām sītā rām rādhē śyām rādhē śyām
śiva śankara śiva śankara śivē śāradē

sūrya-bimba bēre bēre nīrakoḍadi kaṇḍarū
iruva sūrya caitanya śakti ondē
baṇṇa baṇṇada vidyut dīpa halavu bagegaḷiddarū
avugaḷalli hariva vidyut śaktiyu ondē

Though one can see the reflection of the sun in different pots of water, there is only one sun. Similarly, though there might be different electric bulbs, electricity is singular.

vividha rīti ākarṣaṇe ābharaṇagaḷiddarū
avugaḷa mūlādhāra cinna ondē
baṇṇa baṇṇada maṇṇina pātrē halavu
bagegaḷiddarū
avugaḷannu māḍalpaṭṭa maṇṇu ondē

Though there are different gold ornaments, they are all made of gold. Likewise, though there are many clay pots, they are all made of clay.

yēnu mahimē (Kannada)

yēnu mahimē janani ninna dēnu māyeyō?
māyagāḷi namma mēlē bīsi naliveyō?

How glorious your delusive power is! Having cast a spell of delusion on us, are you enjoying yourself?

nammagaḷikē ninnadiddu namage garvanīveyā?
hēraḷa sampatta nīḍi viṣaya sukhake dūduveyā?
elladakkū samayavittu ninnadūra gaiveyā?
ninna nāma smaraṇe koḍadē kattalige taḷḷuveyā?

Why are we so proud of our wealth when it is all yours? Why do you bestow on us so much wealth and thus submerge us further in material pleasures? Why do you make us spend so much time on such matters and thus stay away from you? Why do you make us forget your name and push us into the darkness of spiritual ignorance?

bēḍa tāyē bēḍa ninagananta namanavu
jai bhavāni jai śivāni jagadambikē

O Mother, please do not do that! Infinite prostrations to You, O Consort of Lord Shiva and Mother of the Universe!

vidyā-dhanaveṣṭe iddaru naśvaravē tānē?
ī nijavanariva sumati vismṛtiyā gisuveyā?
ellā sukhavu kṣaṇikaviralu śāśvata-venisuveyā?
nija śāśvata sukhada mārgadinda dūra iḍuveyā?

Isn't all knowledge and wealth transient? Why do you make us forget this truth? Though worldly pleasures are ephemeral, why do you make us feel that they are eternal? Why do you keep us away from the path to eternal bliss?

svārtha buddhi manake tumbi mada-matsara-nīveyā?
dīnadalita sēvemaresi bhōgadeḍege vōyveyā?
parara kaṣṭa aritu neravu nīḍō buddhi kalisu
svarga bēḍa mukti bēḍa prēma bhakti nīḍu

Why do you fill us with selfish thoughts and thus encourage pride and rivalry? Why do you divert our thoughts away from serving the downtrodden and towards worldly pleasures? Please bless us with an attitude of wanting to serve others. I want neither heaven nor spiritual liberation. I seek only pure devotion for you.

www.ingramcontent.com/pod-product-compliance
Lightning Source LLC
Chambersburg PA
CBHW061956070426
42450CB00011BA/3118
9781680377729